Bridges:

Anglo-Japanese Cultural Pioneers
1945-2015

BRIDGES:
ANGLO-JAPANESE CULTURAL PIONEERS 1945-2015
Copyright © Suzanne Perrin & Jeremy Hoare 2015

A catalogue record for this book is available from the British Library

ISBN 978-178456-266-3

First Published 2015 by
Fast-Print Publishing of Peterborough, England.

FastPrint
Publishing

http://www.fast-print.net/bookshop

CONTENTS

INTRODUCTION

Three events were instrumental in bringing about the concept of this book: the Tohoku earthquake and tsunami in March 2011, the book launch at Daiwa Japan House of Professor Nish's book *The Japanese in War & Peace: 1942-48* in May the same year, and an exhibition of photographs called *Bridges* curated by Phillida Purvis at Daiwa Japan House in 1997.

These three seemingly unrelated events were the spur that created the idea for a book of interviews, at a time of re-assessment for Japan and Britain following the combined disasters that befell Japan in March 2011. Realising the wealth of experience to be found in Britain about Japan at the Daiwa book launch, we saw the people who had 'grown up' with Japan since the end of the Second World War. It seemed an appropriate time to take stock of this unique relationship between Japan and Britain, and to find out what drew certain people towards Japan, and from the other side, what drew certain Japanese people towards Britain in their working life. Hence, we took the concept of "Bridges", coming from the inspirational exhibition of the same name at Daiwa Japan House.

The people we have interviewed for this book are all specialists in their own field, and have made considerable contributions to the understanding of Japan in this country, whether in business practices, languages, diplomacy, scholarly works, journalism, music and the arts, or humanitarian projects. They all have a voice that strongly resonates through the decades that has brought together hundreds of people to promote cultural understanding on many levels, and overcome cultural differences between our two countries.

We have discovered fascinating parallel strands running through the different stories that focus on diverse backgrounds, but the unifying aspect is one of generation, covering the latter half of the twentieth century into the twenty-first century from 1945 to 2015, giving 70 years of aggregate experience from ten exceptional people. The rapidly changing socio-economic circumstances of this era has changed our culture, and that of Japan, into a far more complex and closely knit relationship than would have been possible in the preceding age. All the contributors are still actively engaged in their work, excepting one, Professor Bownas, who has been posthumously remembered in this book for his pioneering work in business, language, and cultural understanding.

Without the help and assistance of our contributors, this book would not have been possible, and we acknowledge and give thanks for their time and effort spent in working with us on this project. We have been delighted and surprised at the candour and honesty of the interviewees, their views and personal stories which have illuminated the connections between the people of the United Kingdom and Japan, and even beyond.

We hope that this book will be useful for students and scholars of Anglo-Japanese relations of the current era, and also be enjoyed by the general reader for the breadth of social history and vivid cultural life that has been described in the stories from Japanese, British and European contributors.

Suzanne Perrin & Jeremy Hoare
Co-Authors & Editors
London 2015

THANKS

This book is dedicated to the memory of Professor Bownas, and to all the people interviewed here who have generously contributed their time, effort, and huge knowledge of Japan for this project; we give our heartfelt thanks for their patience and understanding.

We also give thanks to Karen Coe for her insightful editing skills, which have helped to shape the chapters in a coherent form.

BRIDGES:
ANGLO-JAPANESE CULTURAL PIONEERS
1945-2015

SIR HUGH CORTAZZI GCMG

FORMER AMBASSADOR TO JAPAN AND HISTORIAN IN ANGLO-JAPANESE RELATIONS

"I'm neither what you might call pro-Japanese nor anti-Japanese. That doesn't mean to say that I don't attach importance to Japan, of course I do. I attach a great deal of importance to people understanding what makes Japan what it is today.

"But I think we mustn't approach this in a racial, or a nationalistic, or a prejudiced way. I'd like us to approach Japan, and to see Japan as a key factor in the world, which it is, to appreciate its good points and to see where there are problems. But don't let us ever do so in a way which is not at least self-critical."

Sir Hugh Cortazzi GCMG

First connections with Japan

My connections with Japan go back some seventy years, because I first began the study of Japanese in the late summer of 1943 when I joined the Royal Air Force. I'd been at St Andrews University where I had begun a degree course at the age of seventeen; I was there for the best part of five terms before being called up. I'd decided to do French and German, and when I joined the RAF I suppose I was thought of as having linguistic abilities and was therefore sent on a Japanese course at SOAS. I was a willing volunteer because I thought it would be interesting and a sensible way of using my abilities during the war.

I was in India during the final months of the War, then in Singapore for the Japanese surrender, where I arrived with the Tactical Head Quarters 14th Army. I was in Singapore with the British Forces from September '45 until June '46. In Singapore I became involved with a few War Crimes Trials, but was mainly occupied with trying to discover the history of the Japanese air forces in South-East Asia during the war. I did some translation but I'd been trained as an interrogator, and therefore I was doing a lot of my work speaking with Japanese officers who had been members of the air services; one I remember was Lieutenant General Kinoshita, Commander-in-Chief of the Southern Air Army.

At that stage I wanted to go to Japan and saw an opportunity of joining the British Commonwealth Occupation Forces (BCOF) in Japan. One element of BCOF was the British Commonwealth Air Contingent (BCAIR) with its headquarters at Iwakuni. There were three air force stations, manned by the RAF, RAAF (Royal Australian Air Force) and RNZAF (Royal New Zealand Air Force). These were at Iwakuni and Bofu in Yamaguchi prefecture, and at Miho, which was in Tottori prefecture and very near to the city of Yonago.

I first visited Hiroshima in August '46 as I was asked by the commander of the British Air Forces, Air Vice-Marshal Bouchier, to take a senior Foreign Office man to see what remained of the city. He turned out to be Robert Scott (later Sir Robert). I drove him to Hiroshima from Iwakuni in a Jeep and we saw what we could. The place was an appalling sight, nothing around the

Dome; the whole mountainside seemed to be burned; it was horrific. I remember then taking him on to Miyajima, not very far away where we could enjoy one of Japan's most famous beauty spots. Obviously we had some idea about the effects of radiation but I don't think that we or others yet appreciated the damage it could cause. I was greatly moved by the famous book 'Hiroshima' by John Hershey, published by Penguin some time later, which was the first impact of Hiroshima on people. One of my friends in Japan was Mr Ueno Yutaka, who lives in Kamakura; he was in, or near, Hiroshima at the time of the bomb, and he must be nearly a hundred by now! Of course, radiation hits some people badly.

As I was a security and provost officer, I was allowed to live off the base when I was appointed to take charge of the Provost and Security Flight stationed in Yonago in January 1947. I then stayed at *Kaike Onsen* just outside Yamago. It was a fascinating period and I became very interested in Japan and its culture. I determined that when I eventually returned to England, which was towards the end of 1947, I would need to improve my Japanese. I'd already done a certain amount of written Japanese – although I'd been trained as an interrogator I felt that I had to know more. I could read reasonably well, but not as much as I would like, and I also felt very strongly that in order to understand Japan I needed to know more about the culture, history, religion, and so on. So I took a degree in Modern Japanese at SOAS and graduated in the summer of 1949.

Moving to Japan with the British Foreign Office

I'd applied earlier to join the Foreign Service, as it was then called, but was not able to achieve the marks required. So I re-applied in 1949 and achieved the same marking, but fortunately they hadn't got enough candidates with the necessary marks that year and they took me in! I joined what was then the Foreign Office in October 1949, and remember working for my first three months in the South East Asia department. I was posted in January 1950 to Singapore, and served with the Commissioner General's office for eighteen months. I was then posted to Japan, where I arrived in October 1951, and was there from '51 to '54.

On my first arrival in Japan I saw that the infrastructure had been practically destroyed by the air raids. Iwakuni was not exactly obliterated, but there was a lot of damage around the air base, and certainly all the industrial cities.

Attitudes towards Japan

I was fascinated by Japan but I never had any doubts about some of the cruelties of the Japanese forces. I had an uncle as well as a Dutch cousin who suffered as POWs working on the Burma-Siam railway. I was pretty well aware of what went on, also from the War Crimes Investigations in Singapore. It was not just the British and the Dutch who suffered; the people of Singapore, especially those of Chinese origin, had suffered even more, and I understood how much hostility the Japanese had aroused. So, while I was fascinated by Japanese culture, I don't think I ever took a romantic view of all things Japanese. I've never been a particular fan of Lafcadio Hearn, although I admire some of his writings. There is a certain 'Hearn-ism' which has coloured some people's view of Japan and perpetuated false romantic images of Japanese women, Mount Fuji, cherry blossom, and so on.

When I went back in 1951 and joined the Embassy, I found myself up against Japanese bureaucracy, and saw how maddeningly arrogant some of those Japanese bureaucrats could be. So I suppose my attitude to Japan has had its ups and downs; I hope I now take a more objective, reasonable view. I think I do because I don't take the view that you condemn a people, or a country – you may condemn certain actions which said country has done, or said people have done, but I think you treat people as individuals. There are good, bad, and just mediocre people in every country, and so I'm neither what you might call pro-Japanese, nor anti-Japanese. That doesn't mean to say that I don't attach importance to Japan, of course I do. I attach a great deal of importance to people understanding what makes Japan what it is today.

When we consider the behaviour of the Japanese in World War Two, we should not forget there are a number of episodes in our own history which need, as they say, *jiko hansei* – self-reflection. We must try to look at Japan as objectively as possible, because only by doing so can we actually understand it. We mustn't look at other peoples and cultures in racial, nationalistic or prejudiced ways. Only if we suppress such feelings can we understand Japan properly and see Japan as a key factor in the world – which it is; to appreciate its good points and to see where there are problems. But don't let us ever do so in a way which is not at least self-critical.

Japanese nationalism

After the War we were in Germany, from 1958 to 1960. We were in Bonn, and of course I came across ex-Nazis there. Now, I don't want to compare – comparisons are difficult to make – but I do think that the Germans have made more effort, as Ian Buruma and others have written and pointed out, to come to terms with their past. So when I look at modern Japan, I do get worried by the extreme nationalism of certain elements. I don't think we should exaggerate that danger, but I dislike the remarks made by Taro Aso, for instance, about the Weimar Constitution and some of the other things which Japanese nationalists have said publicly. I equally abhor official visits to the *Yasukuni* Shrine.

I used to walk frequently to the Yasukuni Shrine, indeed almost every day from the Embassy, because it was a good walk and I regarded it as a park. I don't think we should necessarily object to a country having a memorial to its war dead, we have our own to our war dead, but we don't memorialise them. You may argue that the War Crimes Trials – (IMTFE, the International Military Tribunal for the Far East) – had made mistakes. I don't think it was entirely objective 'world justice'; there was an element of rough justice in its methods and conclusions. It had to be seen to be done at the time. However, I don't think there can be any doubt about the guilt of most of the people condemned by the court, although probably the condemnation of Mamoru Shigemitsu was an injustice.

That said, I abhor the attempts made by some Japanese nationalists to argue that those condemned by the tribunal were heroes. I regret greatly that the memorial at the *Yasukuni* only covers ex-soldiers, ex-military people. Let's bear in mind that more Japanese died, many more died, as a result of the air raids and by what, in my view, was criminal negligence at the end of the war by the Japanese leaders – they failed to recognise that Japan was defeated, and therefore they inflicted more unnecessary suffering on their own people.

I often debate with myself about Hiroshima and Nagasaki, but I'm not sure that, in all the circumstances, I can condemn the decision, bearing in mind what happened in Okinawa in 1945. I would not have liked to have to go and join, as I might have had to do, an attack on Japan. If it had not been for the bombs inducing Japan at the last hour to accept the Potsdam Declaration, allied prisoners of war in Japan faced a probable massacre. The then-leaders of Japan in their refusal to face up to the inevitability of defeat with what can only be described as criminal irresponsibility inflicted on the Japanese people, avoidable suffering and destruction by adhering in cowardly fear of military extremists to a loyalty which no longer had any real meaning and was certainly immoral. By January 1945 at the very latest it was clear that Japan faced defeat and destruction but they were arrogant, blind, prejudiced and afraid of appearing 'disloyal'. One could argue that these attitudes date back to the ethos of state Shinto and of *Bushido*, so-called code of the warrior.

In Basil Hall Chamberlain's book *Things Japanese,* in the 6th edition, the version published in the west, there's an article on *Bushido,* which describes it as an 'invented religion'. The Japanese censors objected to this description and cut out the pages which dealt with *Bushido* before it could be sold in Japan. So there were two versions of the 6th edition. I've got copies of each edition, including the two versions of the 6th edition. The development of Japanese imperialism is a fascinating subject. Professor Beasley's book on Japanese imperialism *The Rise of Modern Japan*, which I reviewed is a good book. One could argue that Japanese nationalism had its roots in much earlier times. The Unequal Treaties were one excuse, but to blame the treaties for the growth of Japanese imperialism is similar to attempts to justify the rise of Nazism by the Treaty of Versailles.

The re-editing of history goes on today. When I received the *Yamagata Banto* Prize in Osaka I gave a little speech in Japanese to the audience, in which I tried to look objectively at 20th century history. In the course of my speech I mentioned the Nanking

Massacre. Now I have no doubt whatsoever that appalling things happened there. These facts were recognised by important Japanese as having happened. But someone like Watanabe Shoichi, denies it. Well, it's a bit like denying the Holocaust. I don't think anybody will ever know how many people died in Nanking, but that isn't the point. You might just as well say there weren't three million Jews killed in the Holocaust, it was only two and a half, or whatever...

One could go on discussing this, it's an on-going subject, but I think it does emphasise the importance of our attempting to understand the way in which modern Japan developed. We can't ever justify cruelty, but we can understand how it occurred. But this doesn't actually alter the fact that we need to balance the evil against the good. The good are the positive things, and there are many. I have great admiration for Japanese art, Japanese culture, literature, and I believe that we should understand more about them. The war is an important issue, but it isn't the totality – our relationship with Japan is a much broader one, and must be so.

Importance of Japanese studies

I've spent a great deal of effort in trying to work for the expansion of Japanese studies. I don't want to put in too much of the 'I', but when I was Ambassador and I heard from Carmen Blacker that there was a real danger that Japanese studies at Cambridge would end, I did my best. I managed to put a piece into the *Rondan* (London) column of the *Asahi Shimbun* about the dangers and problems, and talked to Mr Hiraiwa of the *Keidanren*. Probably if I hadn't done that it is possible that the *Keidanren* would not have come up with the money, which enabled the Chair of Japanese to be established at Cambridge, and the further development of Japanese studies at the University. I also supported the establishment of the Parker Committee in 1984/85. Peter Parker was an old friend. We had had a number of different reports covering Japanese studies; there was the Scarborough Commission at the end of the war, then the Hayter Report, then the Dainton Committee and the Parker Report. All these have helped but the future of Japanese studies in the UK is not secure. It isn't just a question of language. One of the basic problems is that we don't have a sufficient corpus of Japanese specialists and we don't have enough young British scholars doing Japanese, taking the PhDs. As a result, appointments in Japanese studies are more and more likely to go to foreigners. One issue for young people interested in Japan is what career it will lead to. Some may go into business or banking. In the 1960s, when I was commercial counsellor in the British Embassy in Japan, there were practically no British businessmen who spoke any Japanese at all. It is somewhat different today, but British business leaders are inclined to say, "Everyone speaks English these days; we don't want to recruit linguists; we want people with business experience". Another problem which lies in the university system is that of over-specialisation. If you're a historian, you tend to specialise in an ever-narrower period or aspect.

Modern Japanese Scholarship

This was the problem when I was asked to write a book on Japanese civilization for Sidgwick & Jackson's series *Great Civilizations of the World*. I didn't feel that I was necessarily the right person to do it because I was not an acknowledged scholar, I was an amateur. But there was nobody else who was prepared to take it on. I had an exchange of letters with Donald Keene. I'd just done a review of his latest book and I sent it to Donald, because he has always sent me his books; he's a year or two older than me, and we've known one another for many, many years. He said to me, "Thank you for your review, I suspect that no-one else will, there won't be another review". Which I think is depressing. I'm regarded by some Japanese scholars as a 'populariser'. Donald Keene, who is to my mind, the outstanding living Western scholar on Japan, and there are some very good ones, writes for the general reader as well as for specialists.

You know, it's the sort of people who say, "Oh well, some of the greatest historians…" like I've heard it said of Trevelyan, "Oh, Trevelyan, he's a populariser…" which is nonsense! But if you look at the sort of articles which appear in *The Japan Forum*, the BAJS review, some are, I find, almost unreadable. Well, they're incredibly specialised and very tightly focused on a period or a subject, there's no breadth or relationship. The problem is that modern scholars are looking at matters too much in terms of the detail; they're not able to take an overview. That doesn't apply to someone like Ian Nish, of course, or Carmen Blacker, who was a very old friend of mine. One of the problems, of course, is the development of *jargon*; I've just got this book, which has recently been published, *"Zen Landscapes"*. It's fascinating but really unreadable, some of the sentences! I mean, it's got some beautiful photographs, but I decided I can't review it, because if I have to read a sentence twice, or three times, before I think I know what it means – and I don't think my vocabulary is bad! And then I've had to go back to the Oxford Dictionary to find out what it meant!

It's important that a scholar should be able to access both records in English and Japanese, but it can go too far. Some scholars are such perfectionists, or so PhD-oriented, that they have not or will not produce anything on paper, until they have looked up everything, but it means that nothing gets produced. It's partly the university system that insists on regarding the number of citations of an article as significant. One of the reasons why I sometimes have difficulty in getting people to submit articles for the books I've edited is because they've not been peer reviewed, and therefore they're not regarded as 'citeable' [quotable]. I've met with and talked with many Japanese scholars but not as many as Ian has; Ian has done much more.

It is important to be able to look at historical issues from both sides. For instance the 'unequal treaties' will be viewed differently by British and Japanese scholars based on their readings of the papers available to them. The best scholars will look at as many sources as they can find. They accordingly need a good understanding of both languages. But obviously, if you're picking up a subject like the Treaties, and the beginning of the Meiji period, Japanese scholars are going to be looking at it from a different point of view. If you're looking at the Sino-Japanese War of 1894-95, their view is not going to be the same as ours, it's understandable. We're looking at it from a Western perspective and they're looking at it from a Japanese perspective. That doesn't mean to say that either are right or wrong, but it's a different angle, you can't expect the same angle.

Mrs Thatcher and Japan

For the next volume of *Biographical Portraits* [volume IX published in December 2014] I have drafted a piece about Mrs Thatcher and Japan. It's only got to be about five thousand words, but actually there is an immense amount to say. They were the Nakasone years and I was in Japan when she was Prime Minister. I am neither a 'Thatcherite' nor an 'Anti-Thatcherite', but I have to say that in terms of the relationship with Japan, to put it in the crudest terms, Thatcher was "a good thing". She recognised the way in which the Japanese economy had developed, what Japanese business was doing, and she supported wholeheartedly our attempts to persuade Japanese companies to invest in the UK.

If it hadn't been for her intervention I don't think we would have got the Nissan investment, and that of course lead to Toyota. Honda was already here, but it was a catalyst which brought many other companies here. It was, in fact, a catalyst which re-invigorated the British motor car industry. Now people have criticised Mrs T, and I've done so myself for many things. But I have to say that in terms of Anglo-Japanese relations, although many of the Japanese used to say *"Ano onna!"* (that woman!) they always respected her. The Japanese businessmen respected her, and when I went to Japan in 1980 Britain was suffering from *"Eikoku byo"*, ("British sickness" in the economy), but after Mrs Thatcher you hardly ever heard that word.

Importance of Britain and Japan to each other

Japan is not as important to Britain as it was in 1902 when the first Anglo-Japanese Alliance was concluded. But that doesn't mean that Japan isn't important to us. In 1902 Japan was emerging as the key player in the Far East. Now Japan is not the key player. This is a basic problem about our approach to Japan, our understanding of Japan, and the question of Japanese studies. People are not studying Japan, they're going to China. It's China, China that everyone talks about.

This to my mind is unfortunate and possibly to some extent mistaken, because of course Japan is still the third largest economy in the world. I know it is suffering from various problems including intractable deflation, but it has great things to offer to the world. Japan remains a major power and it is important to us not only in economic terms but also in world politics. Now, the question, "How important is Britain to Japan?" is a different question.

Our importance to Japan, to a very considerable extent, depends on our influence in the world, for instance our relationship with the United States, but also fundamentally our membership of the European Union. So I welcome the Japanese comment that they had been consulted by the British Government and had said that if we left the EU that would have a considerable impact on our relationship; it would indeed! It would impact not only on economic relations; it would also impact on the political relationship. If we turned ourselves into a Norway, or a Switzerland – the Swiss being the most insular country in Europe – you understand what I mean. London has been the most important diplomatic post for Japan in Europe. In the past, pre-War, it was Germany but London was always key; London, Paris and Berlin. Today the Japanese would probably still give a slight preference to London, but for how long? That is why we need to work on our relationship with Japan, including in business and science. This then raises the question of the future of education policy. How good are our universities? Some British universities are still among the best in the world. What about Japanese universities? Inevitably when we consider how many Japanese students come to British universities we run immediately into the problems caused by our fixation on immigration and the stupidities of our immigration policies especially over student visas. We sometimes shoot ourselves in the foot!

The basic problems are caused by ignorance, obstinacy and prejudice – ours and theirs. How many British Members of Parliament today have any knowledge of Japan? Not many. How many Japanese Members of Parliament are interested in Britain? Probably slightly more, but I'm not sure. London is still a key outpost for Japanese newspapers and Japanese papers certainly carry more news about Britain than British papers do about Japan. But the Japanese correspondents don't spend long enough here. Nor do all of them, perhaps because of limited language skills, get out and talk to people. Apart from the *Financial Times*, the *Economist*, and the *Times*, not much appears in the British press about Japan. The BBC, the *Economist*, the *Financial Times* and the *Guardian* have resident correspondents, but coverage is sparse unless there is a disaster.

Internationalisation

'Internationalisation', '*Kokusai-ka*' used to be much discussed in Japan but unfortunately discussion does not lead to much action. The young Japanese are not going abroad as they did in the Meiji period. Then young Japanese came, they wanted to study and learn how to solve some of their problems. Now, do they do this? No they don't. Japanese don't seem to want to live 'abroad' ; they're almost more insular, in that sense, than the British.

There is another problem; why is Japanese English so bad? 'Bad' is perhaps the wrong word, but compare it to say, German English; the Germans who speak English are good at it. Then, one of my favourite topics, why is it that the Japanese women who speak English speak it much better than Japanese men? Donald Keene was saying that he'd been up to Niigata, I think it was, to see a museum which had put on an exhibition of his works, and he noted that there was *nothing* in English! Well, you know in Japanese English, the English is "Japped, *Japlish*"!

I do still think that Japan is a key player in East Asia, in spite of all the talk of China flexing its muscles in the region. It's fundamentally important that Japan should join the TPP – Trans-Pacific Partnership. Its failure to achieve this shows to my mind a fundamental lack of 'internationalisation'. Japanese bureaucrats tend to be inflexible and inward looking. But Japanese businessmen were often not much better. I noticed while I was an adviser to NEC that the Japanese members of staff did not appreciate the importance of good communication and trust between them and their British staff. The Japanese members of staff would talk to one another in Japanese, and therefore those people who worked for them who didn't speak Japanese were left out. To overcome this problem some Japanese companies are now insisting on English as the main language for their work, in view of the fact that English is the international language of business and technology. But is that fair? Is that right? I don't know. How best to deal with local staff is a major problem for companies investing abroad. Do local staff have full access to the head office? Are they members of the main Board? This immediately raises the question of corporate governance in Japanese companies.

We're used to dealing with international relations through our diplomatic service, but they aren't, and Japanese bureaucrats are not flexible. That is true of a lot of Japan.

Obstacles to business

In the 1990s, when I was a consultant and an advisor to various business corporations after diplomatic service, foreign nationals had difficulties in getting into Japan and actually making their mark. Japanese non-tariff barriers remained serious obstacles to doing business in Japan. Unfortunately being an 'advisor' to any company, Japanese or British, can be frustrating if you are an activist like myself, who wants to give advice or do something. Japanese firms tended to want you as a door opener and as a name. So was it difficult enough, even to give advice to British governors too, over Japan. Most people don't like following the advice of others unless it chimes with their own prejudices! Although they appoint people as advisors, they don't actually take any notice.

Japan's position in the future

Is China set to dominate the region or will Japan ever regain its premier position in East Asia? I don't think it can be number one in Asia again. The biggest problem for Japan is going to be, in my view, its declining and ageing population. I am critical of our attitudes to immigration here, but the general attitude to immigration in Japan seems to be, "We don't like them, we don't want them." Japan still hasn't really opened up.

I hope that Japan will continue to maintain its technological edge; that's very important. But look at some Japanese companies; Panasonic is no longer paying a dividend; Sanyo has gone to the Koreans; Japanese scientists at the cutting edge go to America because that's where the funding is, and the research atmosphere ensures that there is scope for development.

Japan is in a difficult situation in East Asia at the moment. To my mind, the biggest problem is the China relationship. If the

Japanese and the Chinese continue to stand pat on their nationalist postures over the *Senkaku* islands, there is a real danger of a spark leading to conflict. The Japanese have not played their hand very well. Japan also has a territorial issue with South Korea and has so far failed to develop the sort of friendly relations with the ROK which should exist between two neighbouring democratic countries. Then there's the problem posed by North Korea, which is a different one. But Japan is important for South-East Asian countries, it's stable and secure. Japan also has another problem not of its own making. It is in a major earthquake zone; it's also a typhoon zone and prone to natural disaster. But there's nothing you can do about that. The Fukushima disaster set them back but I suppose it's also actually acted as a spur.

Anglo-Japanese relations moving forward

So much depends on circumstances; but generally speaking I would have thought Anglo-Japanese relations are on an even keel. I don't think there are many problems, apart from perhaps immigration and visas. There are still non-tariff barriers, but of course it's no longer in our hands, it's really a matter for the European Union, so long as we're a member. Of course if we left the EU – well, let's leave that, those are hypothetical questions and problems.

I think we need to work closely with the international organisations, but one of the problems with international relations is that there are far too few Japanese staff. You look at the UN, the number of Japanese in senior positions is very small. Japanese do not take these posts. You have the exceptions like Sadako Ogata, great people, but you know, they don't put themselves forward. But we will work with them and we must work with them in all sorts of ways.

There are ways in which we can learn from one another in science and technology. There is a range of activities where we can, and should, work together. And I think on the whole that is what we are trying to do on both sides. At the moment there is a reasonably stable relationship between Britain and Japan and this should continue so long as neither of us goes 'haywire'. By 'haywire', I mean for us leaving the EU, or becoming isolationist.

On the Japanese side, following some stupid ultra-nationalist courses. Democracy is, on the whole, reasonably well founded in Japan. There are, of course, all sorts of problems facing democratic institutions in Japan such as the over-allocation of seats to agricultural constituencies. There are of course areas where we differ, for example over capital punishment. I see no reason why our relationship should deteriorate, unless we, or the Japanese, make really stupid moves.

How far have the Japanese weaned themselves off mercantilism? To a very considerable extent, but we'd still like to see more liberalisation in the Japanese economy. Mercantilism is a mistaken policy which is not unique to Japan; it's a view which goes throughout the world; there are still mercantilists in this country.

Japanese Royal family

At the moment I see Japan as remaining a monarchy, as we will remain a monarchy. I don't see any immediate likelihood in either case of moving to a republic for all sorts of reasons, not least of which is who would be president?

But that apart, there are problems in making the monarchy relevant. It seems to me that the present Emperor has skilfully fulfilled his limited role under the constitution. He did very well when he did his broadcast about the Fukushima/Tsunami disaster in 2011. But he's up against the sort of 'seclusionist' element in Japan, which believes that Japan and Japanese emperors are unique, the concept that has gone back from *Jinmu Tenno* to the present time.

Younger Japanese don't show much interest in the imperial institution; there lies a danger. And it won't be easy for the Crown Prince when his turn comes. I translated, as you know, his book, *Thames to Tomo ni*. I certainly much regret that the Japanese have not altered their succession law to allow a woman to succeed. I remember the first meeting I had with the present Emperor in 1953, was just before he came as Crown Prince to London for the coronation of the Queen; he was very young then, so he would have been born before the war and must be in his late seventies now.

Looking to the future on a personal level

I intend to go on as long as I can writing and researching about Japan. It keeps my mind active and alive! But I will be 90 in May 2014 and I do not know how much longer I can hope to continue. Writing is not easy, you have to make an effort; you have to work hard at it. I don't claim to be more than a competent writer or historian. I do believe in sticking at projects! I'm interested in maintaining the *Biographical Portraits* series; Volume 9 is due out at the end of 2014 and Volume 10 I hope will come. My ninetieth birthday coincided with the ninth volume! I certainly will go on doing what I can, and I'm certainly going to carry on working with SISJAC. My latest book for them is called *A Miscellany of Japanese Sketchbooks and Print Albums* (1840-1908), based around fourteen books I've bought over the years; it's basically a picture book.

Editing is a tough business, but that's all right, it's good mental exercise. That's one of the reasons I work on these things, to keep my mind going. You can't keep going solely on the crossword puzzle!

SIR HUGH CORTAZZI GCMG

Former Ambassador to Japan, Diplomat, Historian in Anglo-Japanese relations

	Born in Cumbria, educated at Sedbergh School, St Andrews
1943	Studied Japanese language at SOAS London University; joined the Royal Air Force
1945-6	Sent to Singapore with the British Commonwealth Occupation Forces (BCOF) then to Japan with the British Forces Air Contingent (BCAIR) as interrogator at the War Crimes Trials; demob. 1947 with rank of acting flight lieutenant
1949	Graduated in Modern Japanese Language at SOAS London University; joined the Foreign Office East Asia Department
1951-54	Posted to the British Embassy in Japan with the Foreign Office
1961-65	Second posting to Japan with the FO, then again in 1966-1970
1972-75	Posted to Washington D.C. with the British Diplomatic Service
1975-80	Appointed Deputy Under-Secretary of State in 1975, with various postings in the Foreign and Commonwealth Office service
1980-84	Appointed as Her Majesty's Ambassador to Japan, staying four years
1982-83	Elected President of the Asiatic Society of Japan
1984-91	Appointed Directorship of Hill Samuel & Co, later Hill Samuel Bank
1985-95	Elected Chairman of the Japan Society of London, held position for ten years

1998	Published his autobiography titled 'Japan and Back, and Places Elsewhere'
2000s	In retirement Sir Hugh continued to write and edit many books, publications and literary reviews; translated the account of Crown Prince Naruhito's memoirs of two years at Oxford University entitled 'The Thames and I', 2006
2014-15	Published 'Britain and Japan: Biographical Portraits' Vol IX & X and 'The Growing Power of Japan 1967-1972: Analysis and Assessments' ; continues editorial work on the 'Biographical Portraits' series and publishing new works

AWARDS & HONOURS

1969	Appointed Companion of the Order of St Michael & St George (CMG)
1980	Appointed rank of Knight Commander the Most Distinguished Order of St Michael & St George (KCMG)
1984	Appointed Knight Grand Cross of the Order of St Michael & St George (GCMG)
1988	Awarded Honorary Fellow, Robinson College Cambridge; Honorary Doctorate from University of Stirling,
1991	Awarded Yamagata Banto Prize, Osaka
1995	Awarded Grand Cordon, Order of the Sacred Treasure, (Japan)
2007	Awarded Honorary DLitt University of East Anglia

Sir Hugh Cortazzi at the Oriental Club, London May 1991

PHILLIDA PURVIS MBE

DIPLOMAT, HUMANITARIAN AND NGO WORKER IN ANGLO-JAPANESE RELATIONS

"I suppose it's the fundamental belief that Japan is an enormous – and yet not fully tapped – resource for good in the world. Within its own world, to support the people doing good things in Japan, but also in other countries, Japan could play such an important part.

"So it's trying to help by taking models of good practice and social innovation that I hear of in this country, and in Europe, and sharing it with people I know doing good things in that same field in Japan, trying to help and support them to reach that potential of Japan contributing in the world."

Phillida Purvis MBE

First encounters with Japanese and Japan

In the early 1980s, as I was nearing the end of my Theology degree at Durham University, friends started asking what I would go on to do. One friend was going to take the Civil Service exams in Newcastle and asked me to keep her company. So off I went and found myself taking the Civil Service exams, totally organised by my friend. I managed, to my surprise, to get through each round, and I ended up in the Foreign Office. All new entrants to the FCO do a language aptitude test, which to this day I believe is in Kurdish. I've always had a sort of photographic memory, and as my long-term memory was not being tested I achieved good marks. When the time came for me to be posted, I was told, "You're going to learn Japanese, and go to Japan." I had absolutely no choice in it at all! So it was complete serendipity.

All the FCO language students do a year at SOAS (School of Oriental & African Studies), London University. Originally it was Sheffield University, but they moved it to SOAS in London to be near the Foreign Office. I did this, and a further year at the Japanese language school of the British Embassy, which, up until recently, was in Kamakura, so I lived a year in Kamakura as well. It's a beautiful place, and it was the first time I'd ever lived on my own. Actually I can remember having quite a lot of misgivings. When you learn Japanese in the UK it's all pretty academic, you hardly meet any Japanese people; you carry on living your life in London, and that's what you do during the day. And then to suddenly arrive in Japan... I actually had to part with my boyfriend, and that was rather dramatic.

Before I'd started my language training, I met someone at a dinner party who was learning Chinese with the Foreign Office, and he said, "I live in a remote village, and I have to learn fifty *Kanji* (characters) a day" and I remember thinking, "That sounds really tough, I don't think I could do that!" When I arrived in Narita for my first time ever in Japan, I remember thinking, "O-oh, I don't know if I should be here." I was met by the First Secretary, and as we drove in the car he said, "I don't know if you remember we met at the dinner party of so-and-so..." And I suddenly realised that it wasn't Chinese that the man had been learning – it was Japanese – and I was going to do the very thing that I could recall thinking would be so difficult! So I complained all the way into Tokyo, thinking, "I'm not sure I'm cut out for this! I really don't know..." That First Secretary was David Warren, subsequently the Ambassador in Tokyo, and he reminded me of this story when he became Ambassador!

In fact, if you look at all of the diplomats who have learnt Japanese, Hugh Cortazzi obviously never gave it up, Stephen Gomersall, of course, works for Hitachi, and David Warren is now Chairman of the Japan Society. But not many from the diplomatic service have gone on focusing completely on Japan, as I have done, and I became involved by mistake!

The Diplomatic Corps – Business & NTBs

After I did my language training I started work in the Embassy in Tokyo in the economics section. In those days what we were doing there was economic policy, and our department was involved in persuading Japanese companies to invest in the UK; we were talking to Nissan and Toyota at the time. I helped British importers into Japan, who felt they were being discriminated against by Japanese so-called Non-Tariff Barriers which were called 'NTBs'. We had to make representations to the Japanese government if we received complaints. This was in the early 1980s, when Japan was still under scrutiny for what were regarded as unfair trade practices.

I spent a lot of time on industrial cooperation, trying to get British and Japanese companies to work together, to develop joint products and services or undertake R&D together. It was a very interesting time, although sometimes I felt we were talking at cross-purposes with Japan. For example, the government set up an Office of the Trade Ombudsman, to investigate the complaints raised specifically by foreign importers of unfair treatment in the rules, such as on health, medical or food products, or approaches by customs authorities. As one of the juniors in the Embassy I had to attend the interminable discussions of this OTO, along with representatives of every country which had a complaint, and representatives of every ministry to whom representations were being made. I remember turning up at one meeting; I was twenty-four, and there was not a single woman in the place other than me, they were all much older men. The complaint that I had was from a British importer of calendars, whose calendars were banned from import, on the grounds of their containing nude images. The importer was outraged because he was an artist, and his photographs were, he felt, tastefully obscure and artistic. He contended that the Japanese authorities were being discriminatory against imports since any number of publications of a seriously offensive nature, such as portraying 'S&M', could be bought down back streets in Ueno, Shinjuku or Kanda. He submitted examples as evidence, which I was expected to exhibit at one of these meetings. My waving these bondage pictures before all the men present, and claiming, "You won't let us import *these*, but on every street corner you can buy *these*!" caused huge embarrassment to the Japanese, and the representative of the Policy Agency gravely assured me that they would identify the publishers of the material and put a stop to it. Of course it was complete hypocrisy because everyone *knew* there were many publications available in Japan with comparable images – even *Shunga* violated the government's rules, and it originated in Japan!

So, the Japanese were often to be found paying lip-service to the process of investigating complaints. "Oh yes, we'll address that," they frequently assured us, when complaints were raised, whilst not appearing to notice many of the fundamentally discriminatory practices prevalent at that time. At the same time, I remember representing several British industrial associations – a fork-lift truck association, and ones for machine tools and weighing machines – which were three areas in which the European Union were coming together to make joint complaints. These associations said, "You're dumping goods, and we have evidence that you are selling cheaper in Europe than you are in Japan." And the Japanese thought that was fair game. Of course the boot is on the other foot now, and they're doing the same thing in co-ordination with us against China.

A young female diplomat in Japan

People have often asked me if I felt that I was talked down to, or not treated seriously, because I was a younger woman, but actually it was to my advantage because I could go to these ministries and they would all be rather baffled as to what I was doing there, and therefore be terribly kind to me and take me out to lunch, and tell me, "You don't understand, this is the way it happens." They didn't feel any threat from me, and actually ended up talking to me and explaining things to me, which was extremely helpful. So I did start getting the message. But it was a conflicting one, because I suppose at that time people didn't know how far this economic miracle of Japan would go. They really seriously thought that Japan would take over the world, so everyone was trying to get us to research the mystery of the Japanese *salaryman*, and Japanese industrial practices, which are now so well-known. Now the pendulum has swung so completely; we now know there are other things holding Japan back, but we were all so admiring of them at the time. So it is 'Alice in Wonderland', in a sense, the experience of spending a long time with Japan.

I was young and doing the best I could with the opportunities that were presented. I enjoyed meeting people and had a wonderful time as a diplomat in Japan. I had so many extraordinary invitations as part of the Diplomatic Corps, such as to ride the Emperor's polo ponies, to attend the government's cherry blossom viewing party, and to listen to *Gagaku* imperial court music concerts in the Imperial Palace, not open to the general public. I also travelled to different parts of Japan, with diplomats from other embassies on trade and investment missions, and joined the Ambassador on official visits to various prefectures.

One of my jobs was to represent agricultural importers, which, I recall, involved discussions about importing bull semen and embryos. As a result I got to know the Japan Racing Association quite well, and they invited me to the races, which was great fun. When the JRA heard that I grew up riding, they invited me to ride their horses – an unheard of privilege in Japan. I ended up riding every Saturday in *Baiji-koen* in Setagaya, which the JRA owned, and different ex-racehorses would be saddled up and waiting for me.

Perspectives on ASEAN & Britain

But I knew my posting would only be three or four years, and that another one would be coming up. And in due course I was posted to Singapore in late 1984, where I did political work in Chancery in the British High Commission. But, having been in Japan, I became very interested in how Japan was viewed in the region, although my actual responsibility was to report back to London on the political situation in Singapore and particularly how it affected Britain, and also the importance of Singapore in the region, with the emergence of ASEAN (Association of South East Asian Nations) as a regional network organisation. But South East Asia had this 'look East' policy, and both Malaysia and Singapore did their best to criticise and blame Britain. Their newspapers were full of articles and editorials which implied, "We don't need you, we're looking to Japan ..." as the new important player in the East. So it was quite interesting for me to get that perspective.

I was in Singapore for nearly three years but after that I left the Foreign Office because I got married. I met Christopher in Tokyo. He was there as an investment banker, and he used to come and visit me one weekend a month down in Singapore. I could have stayed on in the Foreign Office, and Christopher was very happy that I should do, but my interest really was Japan by then. I think that studying the Japanese language is the thing that made me most connect with how people think, because so much is reflected in the way that the language is expressed. I studied Mandarin when I was in Singapore, because the Foreign Office gave me the opportunity. It was not to the level of my Japanese, but enough to allow me to make comparisons between them, and I certainly had a head start in having learnt Japanese.

Teaching International Relations in Tokyo

Christopher was still working in Tokyo, so I returned to live there after we were married. For a year I taught International Relations at a university in Japan, and I glimpsed the Japanese education system from the teacher's point of view. It was a private institution called *Hakuo* University and, even in those days before the population began declining, private universities didn't want to criticise any fee-paying students. So it was a joke whenever I tried to do tests, or to tell the students they really ought, at least, to know who the prime ministers of their neighbouring countries were. I would then be hauled in by the president and be reprimanded for telling them off! The only students I found interesting were the ones who piped up and asked questions, then when I admired this display of enthusiasm in the staff room I was told on no account must I tolerate such questioning by 'disruptive' students who must not be encouraged in their 'thoughtless' behaviour. It was good to have had this unexpected experience from a different point of view.

I do strongly believe that what I call my various 'incarnations' in Japan have offered me a range of perspectives on different aspects of society. Because also, I used to go out with Christopher to things where I was the 'banker's wife'. People were polite, but no-one ventured a conversation on subjects in which I was interested, which was a drawback for me, because I wanted to discuss Japanese politics and international relations!

UK-Japan 2000 Group and the Japan Centre for International Exchange

Christopher was sent back to London, so we came back to the UK for a year. However, both of us were keen to return to Japan, and were very happy when he managed to persuade his company to send us back. During our year in the UK I worked at Chatham House, running the secretariat of the UK-Japan 2000 Group, a Wiseman's group established by Prime Ministers Thatcher and Nakasone to create more top-level links between the two countries. It was a successful network which centred on an annual meeting held alternately in the UK and Japan, and certainly created the personal networks as intended. But it was ultimately rather remote from grassroots delivery, in which I was interested, although the subjects debated were topical and interesting.

At that time the Japanese secretariat was in the charge of a dynamic, clever young man called Yamamoto Tadashi, who set up a think tank called the Japan Centre for International Exchange, which he established to be a non-governmental centre for international exchange. Previously the Japanese Ministry of

Foreign Affairs had always been the mouthpiece on foreign connections for Japan, but Yamamoto recognised that it wasn't appropriate for them to always be the mouthpiece, and that the US in particular wanted civil society organisations to network for young business leaders, and do various things. So JCIE responded to the request, especially from the US, for a range of civil society organisations to promote links between business leaders and others in the two countries. US-educated Yamamoto ran this non-governmental face of international exchange, funded by the government for many years, effectively becoming Mr Japanese Civil Society – on *his* terms. Unfortunately there were no others to compete and JCIE took charge of similar exchanges with many other countries, such as Korea and Germany, and the Trilateral Commission, limiting diversity of input as everything was done by this one man.

NGOs

I think Japan arguably was, and to some extent still is, held back by the lack of people who can really hold their own in the international arena, people who can speak sufficiently good English, represent enough opinion in Japan, and engage in meaningful dialogue. Yamamoto played an important part in initiating this valuable NGO and international dialogue, but the Japanese voice, and the range of views which are evident in Japan, were nevertheless little heard in the international forum, as no others took up the baton. Attempts were made to inaugurate a younger person's bilateral group but they, unfortunately, did not prosper. The JCIE was an interesting thing and did serve a purpose at the time, and even today, our relationship could benefit from the ideas of a greater number of more imaginative people.

GAP & LGV in the voluntary sector

Back in Japan I was lucky enough to be awarded a Japanese *Monbusho* scholarship to study at Tokyo University, looking at Japan and ASEAN relations and Japan's role in the resolution of the Cambodian conflict, and how that affected the Japan-ASEAN relationship. Japan's aid-giving is a very significant pillar of Japanese foreign policy, so I became very interested in the question of input of the NGO sector into that aid-making policy.

As a result of this focus, I began to meet quite a lot of interesting new people in the emerging NGO sector.

At the same time, having been at Chatham House, I was approached by two different charities that sent young people to do gap years and volunteering, and they wanted to set up in Japan. I agreed to set up placements for their volunteers, and used to go around community organisations asking if they'd accept young British volunteers. This was the origins of 'GAP' (Gap Activity Projects) in Japan. Many Japanese people at the time told me, "We don't need volunteers, we can afford to pay them." This was 1990, at the height of the Japanese success: "We *pay* people to do things," (in brackets: "If you want to volunteer why don't you send them to Africa or India? You know, places that *can't afford* to pay)."

That really shocked me, because I grew up on volunteering, and thought it didn't matter how wealthy you were as a country, there were things to be done that only people could do by getting engaged. But here and there I met people who understood the benefit of young people's exchange, having young people from a different country, and hearing their views. So I set up quite a few projects, and as a result I later became a Trustee of GAP for more than ten years, and am still very connected with it. But it's changed its name because the GAP clothing company was threatening to sue for the use of the word 'GAP' which they registered and we didn't. So it is called 'Latitude Global Volunteering' (LGV) now.

I'm deeply committed still to young people's volunteering. As I say, you shouldn't be on a board for more than ten years, so I've stood down, but I'm called 'Ambassador' for LGV now. We've made our organisation totally international, and we want to send young people from as many countries as we can. So I'm still in on the track of trying to get Japanese to go and volunteer in Africa, or in other countries.

So these two things – looking for the NGOs in Japan, and meeting people – started my concerns with the voluntary sector. All the time I thought, "I know someone in the UK you'd really enjoy meeting", and that somehow I should make the introductions. I have never in my life thought, "My goodness, what can I do now?" It's always been, "That needs to be done!" and I was capable of doing it, so I'd better do it! I came to know and respect the early leaders of the non-governmental sector in Japan in the 1990s, and desired to help them so far as I could by connecting them to people doing comparable work, striving to meet similar challenges, in the UK and by introducing the fundamentals of our voluntary sector, which had a much longer history.

Japan Centre Study

When I went back to England in the late 1980s, the other major thing that influenced me during my time at Chatham House was my involvement in a feasibility study for a 'Japan Centre'. At that time there was quite a momentum to create such a centre; the Japanese Embassy was right behind it as were Japanese businessmen. But there was a consensus that its feasibility needed to be analysed before progress could be made – how much it would cost, what it would do etc. So I helped pull together that research at Chatham House, and became very engaged with the idea, which I felt would really make a difference, and bring people who knew nothing about Japan into its orbit, spreading the privileged circle who could enjoy its culture. And I never gave up that idea.

At that time I was constantly being contacted by Yoshitoki Chino, who was the President of Daiwa Securities. I knew him because he'd been a mentor to Christopher, as his company was one of the first foreign companies to become members of the Tokyo Stock Exchange. Chino-san was very kind to Christopher, and I used to meet him often – and he, flatteringly, never forgot that I had read a book on *Noh* in Japanese by a favourite author of us both. So he always asked about our research, "Tell me what you're thinking" and "What will it look like?" and "What do you need?" When Daiwa Securities made a donation of £30 million to establish the Daiwa Anglo-Japanese Foundation he wanted it to be the sort of centre we had discussed, a Japanese Centre that was not owned by any one group, but that was a facility and a resource for everybody.

Christopher Everett, a retired headmaster, was head-hunted to lead the Foundation, which launched its scholarship programme, selecting young people because of their potential – it was sort of along the lines of the 2000 Group – young people who were going to go to the top, and sending them for work experience and language training to Japan, well before it moved into its own premises. At the time it cost approximately £1 million for the scholarships and the administration of them, to send *six* Daiwa scholars to Japan every year!

Daiwa Foundation is the biggest funder of Anglo Japanese things, and I was not convinced this was value for money, especially when the JET programme, in which my own daughter participated in 2011, started to send thousands of British graduates to Japan as assistant language teachers. Now the JET scheme – even though it's well reduced – sends two hundred people a year, and they've probably sent around ten thousand British JETs, who are all graduates.

Chino-san had said, "I'll put this money on the table, and I'll see if it will be matched" but the focus was then taken up by the preparations for the centenary of the Japan Society, which became the Japan Festival, and the Japan Centre, being a long-term plan was put on the back burner. Although to be fair a site for it was offered by the British Government, thanks to the intervention of Lord Jenkin, then Chairman of the UK Japan 2000 Group. However the Japanese government felt they could not accept the site, which was located in Hampstead.

At the same time President Chirac of France offered a wonderful Parisian site, near the Eiffel Tower, for a French Japanese centre, since he greatly enjoyed Japanese culture. Japan felt obliged to raise the money to build a centre there, before ever assessing whether it was a good or necessary departure for them. Many argued that there were more compelling arguments for London to be a host of such an enterprise. The London Japan Centre was therefore put on hold; I went back to Japan, the Japanese Embassy diplomats moved on, and no-one emerged to revive the plan.

Daiwa Japan House

When I came back from living in Japan, Chino-san suggested I work in the new Daiwa Foundation Japan House. In 1994, I joined the small team in these new premises to plan a programme for the Foundation.

The programme encompassed the wide range of educational and cultural activities that would promote understanding and connections between Britain and Japan. There was no specific budget for this and within Japan House we achieved a busy programme of seminars, conferences, talks, art exhibitions and cultural demonstrations with limited cost. In the early days, I remember taking in my own china, and stereo system and television for events to keep costs to the minimum! A great benefit was that because Daiwa Foundation was a grant giver, just about anyone around the country planning a Japan-related activity applied to us for funding, so we had a very good network of practitioners to draw on for our events. Wiesia Cook, with whom I worked and who managed the grants programme, had an amazing memory for this purpose and very perceptive 'antennae', and we were able to make all sorts of connections and draw on the skills of many people as a result.

Our very first exhibition of artists was the work of Alan Graham Dick, and he helped me cook up the strategy for my idea for an exhibition called 'Bridges'. Building on our exhibition programme, and the goodwill of the participating artists, we organised a touring exhibition which was set up at unusual venues all around the country. The 'Bridges' exhibition set off to schools, factories, offices and community buildings in 1997, and eventually continued for two years because we also took it to Japan. This certainly was achieved on a shoestring as the artists all brilliantly helped to set up, take down and transport the work, and gave talks and educational workshops on a voluntary basis. As intended we managed to tour the show to places that other cultural events didn't reach, and we had huge fun, and impact, in the process. We definitely achieved one of the Foundation's objectives – to stop being so London-centric!

As far as I could, I tried to make a great resource of Japan House for any person or group involved in Japan-related, noncommercial activity, but it was not the most versatile space for all purposes. I always aspired to that original dream of inclusivity, but by then, the name Daiwa had been attached to every activity and programme of the Foundation, so no other funder could consider contributing. I hoped that Daiwa Japan Foundation's house would be used as a resource. I hoped that any group that was doing a Japan-related activity, that we knew and trusted, could use the premises any time of the day or night. But as soon as I left that was stopped, and it was run on a more formal basis. It does very good seminars, but the physical space is not very flexible. As to the achievements of that time, the fact that there were people coming in and out all the time using the premises, and there was a buzz about doing things related to Japan, and networking with people, and trying to tell people, "Oh, you're doing that, have you heard of someone doing *that*?" and really trying to make it a hub. I like to think there was a buzz about the place, and that was fun, and we did have an enjoyable time.

Eric Roll, our Chairman, always gave me encouragement, since I had known him for years. When I finally left, he promised Daiwa would always do their best to support any of the civil society exchanges I was then dedicated to organising, on the common social challenges facing our two societies. One big project I put together was on homelessness, and I took homeless charity leaders to Japan to exchange with counterparts there. Unfortunately Daiwa did not support this, but commitments had been made so I had no choice but to fund it myself, with some support from the British Council.

Leaving Daiwa

We all thoroughly enjoyed those days at Daiwa, but more and more I realised there are so many people doing wonderful cultural things, but no-one else was particularly interested in working in civil society exchanges, which was my interest. So this thought prompted me to leave and set up my own organisation, Links Japan, in 1998, to focus on this area.

Voluntary Sectors

In the early days I was really trying to help Japanese young voluntary organisations understand how our voluntary sector worked: What was the relationship with Government? How did you fund raise? What were the issues of accountability? How did you get public support? There were varieties of donations that were very structural, and those were the issues that we were exploring. On the structure of building voluntary sector areas in civil societies in Japan, definitely Britain is guiding Japan. However, events started moving on to issues like care of the aged, and I've done a lot around employment of people with disabilities.

You know, when you start looking at areas in which dynamic people are working, there are always ideas that people have that we can mutually learn from, that we don't have, so there is always value in two-way exchange and sharing. It has tended to work out that I initiate, devise and fund raise for projects that go to Japan, generally speaking, although sometimes I'm invited to bring voluntary-sector experts to participate in specific events. One of my trips to Japan in 2011 focused, for example, on the tenth anniversary of the International Year of the Volunteer. I was asked to invite some foreign speakers, and I agreed to help, "provided they're not from Europe or the U.S." as a lot of people have opportunities going from there, so I found a Lebanese, a Congolese and a Brazilian, and organised them, told them what it was about, and what we were trying to achieve. They all kindly then agreed to stay on for two additional touring programmes, that took us down to Kyushu, speaking on social innovation and Japan/Africa community-based partnership building. My other NPO agreed to arrange other seminars and we spoke about the development of social enterprise and international connections at those events.

In the early days when I set up, the Internet was brand new, and people couldn't easily find out about voluntary organisations in the other country, and that's what I felt I could help with at that time: find out who were the voluntary organisations. And I could speak to them, write to them in Japanese, and so on. Otherwise in those days – we could hardly imagine it now – but you'd have to look up in a telephone directory, try to find a number, and say could you send me your annual report or some other literature, then I'd have to have an exchange by fax with Japan at difficult hours, so it was all immensely laborious. I feel that now the Internet does exist, people are able to find out this sort of information for themselves. E-mail has just opened up all sorts of possibilities in terms of speed and volume of communication, and this has made a huge difference to delivery of outcomes.

BCS & Reconciliation

When I was in Singapore I first heard about the Burma Star Association because it was the fortieth anniversary of the end of the Second World War and loads of POWs were paid by the British Government to come out to Singapore. We had to organise for them to go up the Burma Railway, or to where they had been, and I ended up spending a lot of time talking to them. And of course, when they knew I had a connection to Japan, they had a lot to say about the Japanese. Also, when I first went out to Japan, I remember friends of my parents saying, "Why do you want to go to Japan?" So I did naively announce when I got there, that I'd really be interested to understand how we've talked to the Japanese about what happened, so that I could learn from the processes that have obviously gone on, because the subject was always being raised. It still is an issue in the UK, and in the early 1980s it certainly was. The reaction I met with was, "No, that's the past, we're looking to the future."

And then I suppose organising, as I did at Daiwa Foundation, and later, independently in Japan, exhibitions of drawings by the FEPOW war artist, Jack Chalker, and meeting many veterans played a part. There was an organisation called the Burma Campaign Fellowship Group, who were British and Japanese veterans of the Burma War; we gave them a grant from Daiwa, and I ended up on their committee, but then they decided to close down. And I thought that there were still enough "Old Boys", as I call them, the veterans, who would be prepared to talk about their experience, and we shouldn't just stop if there was any will to continue. For me it's about getting on the record what actually happened, from first-hand accounts as far as possible, and otherwise academic analysis of those first-hand accounts.

So with a British and Japanese Burma war veteran I founded the Burma Campaign Society – and we held many discussion meetings with veteran speakers. Most recently I helped to organize a conference at the White Rose East Asian Centre, which is a collaboration of Leeds and Sheffield Universities. I invited the speakers from Japan, China and Korea and raised the money for it. A few years back, while I was at BCS, I did a big seminar at the Cabinet War Rooms around this reconciliation subject to celebrate the 60th anniversary of the end of the War, which was a great success, not least because it was part Lottery funded and we ended up in surplus by about two and a half thousand pounds, which was lovely!

Anyway time goes on, I stood down when I'd run BCS for five years. You know, I did all the mailing and the photocopying, the newsletter, and everything, and when the old boys couldn't really do the discussion meetings I thought, "Look, I've done that." I'm still involved in reconciliation, as secretary of the International Friendship & Reconciliation Trust, and we organise an annual service of reconciliation at Canterbury Cathedral. This year is the 70th anniversary of the end of the Second World War so the service will be particularly special.

Reflections

I suppose my constant focus is the fundamental belief, because of all the wonderful Japanese people that I know, that Japan is an enormous – and yet not fully tapped – resource for good in the world. Japan could play such an important part within its own world, and also in other countries, by supporting the people doing good things in Japan. But they just don't have the personal networks internationally that we take for granted in this country. So it's by trying to help, by taking models of good practice and strategy and social innovation that I hear of in this country and Europe and more widely, and sharing it with people I know doing good things in that same field in Japan, that I'm trying to help and support them to reach that potential of Japan contributing in the world. My latest mission is to try to connect Japanese communities with Africa, so watch this space!

PHILLIDA PURVIS MBE

Diplomat, Humanitarian and NGO Worker in Anglo-Japanese Relations

1970s	Degree in Theology at University of Durham
	Joined Foreign Office and sent to study Japanese at SOAS
1981	Posted to Japan, first to British Embassy language school, Kamakura, then to Embassy Economic Section
1984-86	Posted to Political Section, British High Commission, Singapore; studied Mandarin
1986-87	Lecturer in International Relations at Hakuoh University
1988-89	Secretary to the UK Japan 2000 Group at Chatham House
1990-92	Researcher at Tokyo University in Japanese Foreign Policy; Established placements for young British volunteers in Japan, through Gap Activity Projects served on the board of GAP, later Lattitude from 1998-2010 and Project Trust
1993-98	Deputy Director of the Daiwa Anglo-Japanese Foundation in London
1997-98	Initiated and ran 'Bridges' exhibition, Daiwa Foundation Japan House and its UK and Japan tour
1998-99	Executive Director of the UK-Japan 21st Century Group
1998	Founder Director of 'Links Japan' to promote exchange and learning between voluntary sectors
2002-07	Co-founder and Honorary Secretary, the Burma Campaign Society, promoting wartime reconciliation, (formerly committee member of the Burma Campaign Fellowship Group)
2006	Founded Japan Arena, a charity to establish a Japanese cultural and community centre in London

2007   Honorary Secretary, the International Friendship and
        Reconciliation Trust

2011   Helped establish the Rose Fund in Tohoku, in 2011,
        which disburses to victims of the earthquake and
        tsunami donations made to the Japan Society

2015   Continues to work, as activist and charity trustee in the
        NGO sector, with a special focus on Africa, including
        founding and running a solar lighting initiative –Solar
        Links, in Uganda and South Sudan, and in
        international exchange between civil society
        organisations worldwide, especially between the UK
        and Japan.

HONOURS

2006   Awarded the Member of the Order of the British
        Empire for services to Anglo-Japanese relations

Phillida Purvis with Solar Lighting project in Uganda 2015

PROFESSOR IAN NISH CBE

SCHOLAR IN JAPANESE HISTORY AND ANGLO-JAPANESE RELATIONS

"Let it be said: the problems of contemporary East Asia are many and relevant to Britain, even though we are geographically separated by great distances.

"There are plenty of issues, many of them delicate and sensitive, which deserve international study and dialogue. When you are building bridges between societies, it is essential to have a solid academic base."

Professor Ian Nish CBE

"They chose me. I didn't choose them."

In 1945 I was in the army, in India, and the opportunity arose to be recruited for a Japanese language course. They chose me. I didn't choose them. They chose me because at school I had learnt French, German, Russian – and Russian was the one that they were interested in. They thought it was a difficult language, and Japanese was a difficult language, and required someone with language experience.

Initially I took the view that I was a grammar school boy, and getting into the army was a new life experience. The thought of '24/7' language study for eighteen months didn't appeal very much. But they pressed me and so this 18 year-old joined what was called the School of Japanese Instruction in Simla, and before it moved to Karachi, I was appointed the librarian of the course. So, in a way, that was my first knowledge of Japan and its literature. I graduated in July '46. I was one of a group of about 15, whose first posting was to Singapore, to what was called The South East Asia Translation and Interrogation Centre (SEATIC).

Translating in Changi

SEATIC, as its name implied, was for translation and interrogation; part of the time I was used for interrogating in Changi jail, and part of the time I was translating in headquarters. I was involved in translating the diary of Colonel Hayashi, who had been a commanding officer in the *Kempeitai* in South East Asia. I didn't have a biography of him, what he'd done, whether he'd killed people or whether he'd burnt a village or whatever. But the general assumption was that his diary would contain lots of revelations about the war. Well, I don't think it did. People don't write diaries in their best handwriting, so we would ask the colonel, who was present, "Tell me what you are writing about here", and very often it was about his health and personal matters of that kind. We did an honest job and translated what we could. I was one of a team, I would do a passage, and the next table would do a passage, and so on. I really never discovered what happened to the end product.

The other aspect of our job was to go into Changi jail. It was rather like a drama, a scene from a Japanese drama on the television from the *Tokugawa* period, with lots of *Samurai* sitting cross-legged and bowing. These were fairly senior officers but they were not interrogated by us, we dealt with quite junior people. We were given a list of questions to ask them, mainly along the lines of "Where were you in December 1941?" "Had you any experience of being trained for Malaya and Singapore?" and "How had you come to Singapore?" and so on.

We had been told that in the British Army, we should, if captured, disclose our 'Number, Rank and Name' only. Of course this was peacetime so it was slightly different, and on the whole they wanted to get back home as soon as possible so they were quite talkative. We wrote down their details, but we were not judging them morally, we were just interested from the intelligence point of view. We were building up a picture of how their units from China had been transferred to South East Asia and what sort of training they'd had. So our attitude towards the Japanese was a businesslike approach.

Sailing from Singapore to Japan

I was very lucky that, after two or three months on translation, I was posted to Japan and that meant sailing from Singapore to Kure. There were two sets of people on the ship: the first were senior Japanese officers who had come aboard in Singapore and were going to Sugamo in Tokyo for the War Crimes Trials. Since I was the only one on board who knew Japanese, the master appointed me as interpreter. I was not in charge – the crew members had to take responsibility for the Japanese – but I acted as a sort of middle man.

The second hold was occupied by Chinese nationals who had collaborated with the Japanese in Burma. In other words, the Japanese had, during the war, recruited Chinese to do manual duties, sometimes as drivers. Whether it was compulsory or not I don't know, and the understanding was, whether true or not, that these collaborators were destined for court of law and in KMT (*Kuomintang*) China. They mutinied and tried to break down the hatches when the ship got to Hong Kong, but they did not succeed in getting off the ship. And we did in fact take them as far as

Shanghai and they disembarked there. But I have never tried to follow up the story, and I don't know what happened to them.

Hiroshima

In my book *The Japanese in War & Peace* I describe a visit to Hiroshima which I made soon after I reached Japan. It was fourteen months after the bomb was dropped and naturally, one wanted to visit there as soon as possible. I've reflected on the atomic issue quite a bit, but I don't think that I had a tremendous sense of guilt. I know some people, particularly Americans, did feel much guilt, but the way I've dealt with it in my mind is that Pearl Harbour was an atrocity, Hiroshima was an atrocity, and in between there were lots of atrocities. So, I didn't feel inclined to photograph the damage because I just thought that was in bad taste. I was deeply sympathetic about the deaths and casualties caused, but I'm unhappy about the way that Hiroshima has exploited the bomb as a sort of tourist attraction.

Australian attitudes towards the Japanese in the late 1950s/ early 1960s

After graduating from SOAS in History, I had an appointment at the University of Sydney during 1957-62. The attitude towards Japan there at that time was interesting as it was very mixed. On the one hand you had the RSL – the Returned Servicemen's League – which is like our British Legion, except that it was more hostile towards Japan. This was a time when the Japanese were not popular. Commerce was gradually returning to Australia and the Japanese had already taken up their passion for golf, and wanted to join Australian golf clubs, but they were sometimes blackballed; that was one extreme.

The other side was that I had dealings with the equivalent of Chatham House, the Australian Institute of International Affairs, and their line was that Japan is 'the near north' – not 'the far east'. This was an interesting concept, really, and quite a far-sighted one, because Australia's economic interest was to promote trading connections with Japan. This was as early as the late 1950s and already there was a considerable trade in Australian coal, iron ore, and scrap metal. It was tremendously profitable, so the

Government was rather in favour of developing trade with Japan, and concluded a trade agreement in 1957 between Japan and Australia.

So, my impressions of teaching Japanese Studies in Australia were that I thought the students were very cordial and really very interested in Japanese studies, more so than in Britain. There were large classes on Japan and China; I mean of hundreds of students.

Post-War Japan and Britain

I returned to teach in LSE in 1962. I had left a decade earlier and it was more preoccupied with China than with Japan, because Britain had taken the tremendous gamble of recognising Communist China, an act which America disapproved of. The 1950s were a period of difficult relations between Britain and Japan, but by the end of the fifties Japan was in the United Nations, was in the WTO (World Trade Organisation) and was accepted within international institutions.

In the 1960s relations between Britain and Japan greatly improved. Until then Britain was still too close to the war and British opinion strongly reflected wartime attitudes. It was said that while Japan was trying to understand Britain, Britain was not so assiduous in trying to understand Japan. Japan, locked in a pacifist constitution, was content to be an isolated country relying on the support and protection of the United States. But she was able to join the United Nations and the WTO and was welcomed into many international organisations.

All this time Japan was changing. For two decades after the war she was dependent on the US and signed up to the enduring American-Japanese Security Pact, first in 1952 and later in 1960. But with her spectacular economic growth after the Olympic Games in Tokyo 1964, her place in the world changed. The question now was how soon Japan would return to being an international great power as she had been in the 1920s and 1930s. I remember that I was incautious enough to agree to write an essay in 1967 entitled *Is Japan a Great Power?* It created quite a stir in Japan, but not, I hasten to add, outside Japan. Many of my academic friends surprised me by taking the line that they did not want Japan to become a great power. They wanted Japan to be an unobtrusive country on the world stage which would concentrate on her economic recovery. Her prosperity has, of course, grown since then. It has led to export surpluses and unpopularity abroad. But the same question about Japan's place in the world still continues to arise and divide Japanese thinking. At a popular level there is still a strong streak of pacifism and reluctance to participate in overseas enterprises unless they are connected with aid or linked with United Nations' action.

This economic change affected Britain's attitude to the country. After the war Britain took an attitude towards Japan which was subtly different from that of the United States, probably because Washington had been closer to Japan during the Occupation years (1945-52) and had come to admire and respect her. British opinion was more affected by issues like the treatment of prisoners of war and the return of trade rivalries of the pre-war period. Over the years London's attitude changed. Around about the symbolic visit of the Queen to Japan in 1975, Britain began to manifest an admiration for Japan's spectacular post-war achievement. In some ways it resembled the admiration which British people felt in the Victorian era towards the *Meiji* (1868-1912) Japanese for their capacity to reorient themselves in a western mould. This did not mean that there were no disputes between their governments over Japan's successful export record. These disputes were serious and were exacerbated by the fact that the British economy, and indeed those of most of Europe, seemed to stay stagnant for so long. Japan's sustained level of high economic growth, however, won the admiration of the City of London; and her investments in the British economy in the 1980s were much needed and much appreciated. But happily Japan and Britain now find themselves sharing many of the same political objectives in the international sphere.

Teaching Japanese studies in the UK

My duty at LSE from 1962 was to teach Japanese history in its international setting from the nineteenth century onwards. As a country Japan faces two ways: towards the Pacific Ocean and towards the Asian continent. In the first context she had always to pay attention to her maritime resources and measure herself against the great naval powers, initially against European powers, then against the US Pacific fleet and more recently against China. In the second context the overwhelming problem has been the relationship between Japan and China since 1850, an issue as relevant today as it has always been.

Outside LSE the problem was to promote Japanese studies in the UK as a whole. There had of course been government reports on the place of Japan in British academia, like those of the Scarbrough (1947), Hayter (1961) and Parker (1986) committees. There were broadly two categories involved: the small group of language-teaching schools, at the universities initially of Oxford, Cambridge, SOAS University of London and later Sheffield. A larger group of campuses dealt with Japan as part of world history, the first Great Power to come from Asia. These included most of the larger metropolitan universities. Class numbers in the former tended to be small; in the latter large. Staff and students in both categories were brought together in the British Association of Japanese Studies (BAJS) founded in 1974. Their annual conferences have been a great stimulus to the growth of research in the field.

The situation was transformed with the inauguration of the Japanese Foundation by the Tokyo government in 1973. It has, ever since, given awards to individuals and organisations working in the academic, artistic and cultural aspects of the Japanese field. In its wake came other grant-giving bodies, most notably the Daiwa Anglo-Japanese Foundation, the Great Britain Sasakawa Foundation and the Japan Foundation Endowment Committee. Together, these made it possible for students of Japanese affairs at all levels to visit Japan more readily. Graduate students and teachers were able to take advantage of studying Japan at first hand and the institutions concerned also benefited. Japanese funding from these quarters assisted greatly at a time when British universities were in financial difficulties.

Japanese and British approach to history

In order to re-examine the relationship between Japan and Britain over the centuries, the Japanese government set up the Anglo-Japanese history project in 1995. This was a joint project in which Japanese and British historians re-interpreted their histories for each other and the general public in order to disentangle any unnecessary misunderstandings. I became one of the general editors of the long series of five volumes entitled *The History of Anglo-Japanese Relations, 1600-2000* which emerged from it. I was an enthusiastic supporter of the project because I believe that we in the West should read and hear much more about what the Japanese say about their history. One aspect is that there should be more translations of current Japanese writings. For example, International House in Japan has started a press which is translating what they consider to be essential works of Japanese scholarship for the Western world. Speaking as a historian, I think that creates problems in itself, but I think the idea is good and we would like to know what is being said at the frontier of research in Japan. In science I believe that there isn't a problem since science is much more global, as so many Japanese scientists have been trained overseas. But that does not apply to the history field where there are inevitably problems over interpretation. The Anglo-Japanese history project was completed with cordiality. We found that we had a good deal of common ground, though we both recognised that there would continue to be areas of sensitivity.

Changes in research

When I retired in 1991, I felt grateful for what those in the field of Japanese studies in British universities had achieved in spite of financial constraints and institutional difficulties. Although Japanese studies in British universities are small by comparison with those in the United States (for example), they are considerable and have achieved a lot. There is a good coverage between universities in the regions. There is also a fair spread in research between the various disciplines and cultural studies, including literature and art, are not neglected. This sounds dreadfully complacent and self-satisfied, and, you know, two people can look at the same document and come out with quite different interpretations! But let it be said: the problems of contemporary East Asia are many and relevant to Britain, even though we are geographically separated by great distances. There are plenty of issues, many of them delicate and sensitive, which deserve international study and dialogue. When you are building bridges between societies, it is essential to have a solid academic base.

Later I retraced my footsteps in Japan between 1946 and 1948 and published a memoir under the title *The Japanese in War and Peace*, including some wartime papers I had collected. I started the work not in 1945, the date favoured by many authors, but in 1943 in order to see what views the Japanese were expressing as national objectives during the war years. In other words they still saw victory as a possibility. But they were conditioned to think that. You could liken that to North Korea recently; you get a mindset, and you have to comply with the mindset. And I believe there was that element in Japan at that time.

Changing international relations

Britain's attitudes have partly been influenced as the result of Japanese donations to British universities in the 1970s, for example STICERD (Suntory and Toyota International Centres for Economics and Related Disciplines) here at LSE. Our universities were in financial difficulties in those days and the Japanese were very generous in their help. I think the same could be said of the Japanese and the car industry in this country. In a way they were more generous in their approach to the car industry than the Chinese are being at the moment.

Now, if you look at the broad spectrum of foreign policy nowadays, Britain and Japan are at one on a wide range of subjects; only on whaling and (dare I say it) whisky are we at odds from time to time. Both countries are partners of the United States. The Japanese have had a Security Treaty with the US since 1952 and a close relationship. Britain by contrast relies on what she calls the 'special relationship' with Washington. While they are both members of the American 'camp' in world affairs, that does not prevent them both from having serious disputes and disagreements.

Japan and Britain have a very close accord in many areas. We collaborate a lot in aid-giving in Africa, because the Japanese sometimes lack the experience in giving in these countries, so there is room for mutual collaboration. Whether it really matters to Britain or whether it matters to Japan to have this tie, I'm not so sure. In a way, Britain to America, and Japan to America, these are the important axes. I think Anglo-Japanese relations are pretty stable, though how can we predict?

The rise of China

Despite the rough and tumble of world politics, Japan has stayed in the American camp since she entered into the US Security Treaty in 1952. Technically she is not an ally; she is a partner. This will continue so long as Japan has worries about her neighbours. In the past three decades there has been much talk of Japan's worry over 'the rise of China'. Of course, the rise of China with her vast population is nothing new. Indeed, in the 20th century Japan assisted China to develop her rich resources, resources which Japan herself lacked. At that stage China was held back by regional and personal rivalries and malfunctioning political institutions. It was pretty clear that after the war Japan recognised the presence of a developing China from the time when Prime Minister Tanaka went on a mission to Peking in 1978 and led the way to signing a number of treaties between the two countries. That a nuclear China poses a threat to Japan goes without saying. How far the new Japan can accommodate the expanding ambitions of the new China, with its spectacular economic growth, only time will tell.

Japan was once the leading nation in East Asia, but is not at that strong position any longer. I certainly think that China is set to keep its dominance. Japanese have said to me that they're worried about the next generation, the sort of late teenagers, and that they lack dynamism. They're energetic enough, but... Whereas the Chinese – in spite of the Communist regime, and the party membership and all these considerations which we think are a bad thing – they still have this tremendous dynamism and entrepreneurship.

We have 850 Chinese students studying economics at LSE, and we have about 420 Japanese students. It is significant in a way and disappointing in a way. And the Chinese, in my experience, speak very good English. To take one case: Africa. Chinese entrepreneurs are busy in Africa – what does Japan do? Japan is active in Africa, but through Mitsubishi, the *zaikai*. That's not the best way to create a new restoration of Japan's fortunes. I think it was overdone, when it was said that Japan would dominate the twenty-first century. We all had expectations of that; I think I had that too, and Britain is the beneficiary of these expectations, and they invested considerably in Britain.

Japan's struggle with internationalism

I think it's true that Japan has a problem with internationalism. I'm rather persuaded with the attitude of Professor Dore, who said quite early on that, "Japan has a class who deal with international matters", meaning diplomats, or perhaps business people if you like. Many people in Britain for example – and this is Ronald Dore's idea – seeing these people think what an internationalised society it is, and he said, "Don't you believe it!"

Japan has very strong national roots. Now, I think one has to refine that. You're only seeing a small section of people who are trained to be international; it's a very small section of the whole population. Having said that, I do feel that Japanese newspapers are remarkably global in their coverage, and I think that if people conscientiously look at television they will see quite a lot of international coverage. But I think on the whole many Japanese, especially young people, are surprisingly blind to international things.

Looking to the future

Looking to the future, I am hoping shortly to complete a book in the field of Sino-Japanese relations. This takes me away from the field of Anglo-Japanese relations in which I have been labouring for many years. In the words of some critics, too many years!

Because my career has been inextricably linked with Japan, my wife Rona married Japan as well as me. She was originally a teacher in the University of Aberystwyth in a totally different subject and our honeymoon in Japan in 1966 was her first immersion in the country. On a personal basis, we have a fairly large circle of Japanese friends with whom we keep up correspondence, my wife more than me. She exchanges Christmas cards and New Year greetings with a large number of Japanese ladies and will continue to do so as long as we are not bankrupted by the postage! I have been lucky, since I retired, to have received invitations to visit Japan once every two or three years. We last went there in November 2010 for me to give a lecture to the Japan Academy. But I think that we're more or less reconciled to the fact that we've paid our last visit to our second favourite country. We don't expect to go back. Sad, but it's a funny feeling.

Professor IAN NISH CBE

Scholar in Japanese History and Anglo-Japanese relations

	Born in Edinburgh, Scotland
1945	Selected to study Japanese at the Army School of Japanese Instruction, Simla and Karachi
1946	Posted to SE Asia Translation and Interrogation Centre (SEATIC) in Malaya – Changi
1946-48	Sent to Kure W Japan HQ Combined Services Interrogation Centre as translator
1948-57	Gained degrees in History at Edinburgh and in Japanese History at SOAS, London
1957-62	University of Sydney, teaching Japanese history
1962-91	London School of Economics, International Relations Dept Japan specialist; wrote monographs on *Origins of the Russo-Japanese War* and *Japan's Struggle with Internationalism*
1978-80s	Secretary (later President) of the British Association for Japanese Studies (BAJS)
1985-8	President of the European Association for Japanese Studies (EAJS)
1991	Retired as Professor Emeritus of International History, London School of Economics
1995	Appointed one of the general editors of the Anglo-Japanese history project, resulting in *The History of Anglo-Japanese Relations 1600-2000* in five volumes
2001-02	Two volumes of collected writings were published simultaneously in Britain and Japan
2011	*The Japanese in War and Peace, 1942-48* published by Global Oriental
2012	Statistical overview of writings by and about Professor Nish (OCLC/World Catalogue) encompass more than

200 works in over 300 publications in four languages and over 7,000 library holdings

Google postings for 'Ian Nish Japan' gave more than 164,000 results

2015   Continues to work on editorial and research projects on Chinese and Japanese international relations

HONOURS

Conferred Commander of the British Empire

1991   Conferred Order of the Rising Sun, Gold Rays with Neck Ribbon

1991   Japan Foundation Award

2007   Honorary Member of the Japan Academy

London School of Economics, Houghton Street, London

SIR GEOFFREY BOWNAS CBE

(9TH FEBRUARY 1923 – 17TH FEBRUARY 2011)

WIESIA COOK BOWNAS

WIDOW OF PROF. GEOFFREY BOWNAS

"His favourite place, he talked about the "Kyoto effect", in his poetry he talks about Japanese aesthetics; for Geoffrey the sounds of Japan were very important.

"I think he [Geoffrey Bownas] fostered the knowledge of Japan in so many ways, not just as a scholar, but also in the business context. He was a person of many parts, and the importance of linguistics and cultural skills in this economic context, I think, was his most important contribution."

Wiesia Cook Bownas

First meeting with Professor Bownas

I first met Geoffrey in 1994 when I was working for the Daiwa Anglo-Japanese Foundation in London, where I would work until 2002. He was one of our speakers at a seminar, 'Managing across Borders: Culture and Communication Issues for British and Japanese Businesses', and was chairing a talk on 'Partnerships with Japan on Major Projects Worldwide'. I helped him with the preparations for the talk – the logistics, preparing the lecture room etc. He wanted to say 'thank you' so he asked me to dinner! We thoroughly enjoyed talking, and he asked me to have dinner with him again and we took it from there.

He was Professor Emeritus of Sheffield University and semi-retired from working in the business field; he was also working for *Gyosei,* the Japanese University in Reading, and did a lot of other things including writing and translating. He was sitting on various bodies, including chairing the lecture programme for the Japan Society, and he was a Vice President of the Institute of Linguists and an advisor to the JET Programme among other things. As often happens, he was always busy in retirement and yet very generous with his time in giving advice and help to other people.

From codebreaking to Confucius

What Geoffrey had with his life was slices of luck which made a wonderful cake. One slice of luck was how he came to be breaking Japanese codes at Bletchley Park. It was by coincidence: on parade, one cold March morning, the sergeant came out and wanted five volunteers to learn Japanese. Obviously nobody volunteered, and the sergeant was one of those who went, "You, you, you, you and *you!*"

When Geoffrey was in Oxford studying Classics, he received a grant to go to China to study Chinese, but the Revolution prevented him from going so he never went. Rather than wasting the money, it was decided to send him to Japan, to study in Kyoto with Professor Kaizuka Shigeki (1904-1997), the foremost expert on China. And that's where his whole life changed.

He went there by cargo ship from Southampton, via Genova, and on to Japan where he arrived in Kobe on 1ˢᵗ November 1952 and then to Kyoto. Professor Kaizuka Shigeki was the most inspiring teacher he ever had, he always talked about *Kaizuka-sensei*, and said that he owed him so much. He studied with him from 1952 to 1954, and his first job was to translate Confucius into English.

He was very lucky because he was living in a *hanare*, a big western-style house, on the outskirts of Kyoto, a place called Fukakusa, which had a proper flush toilet. So in the neighbourhood there was a *gaijin* living in the house, and obviously with a western style toilet. They would wait for him to pull the chain and listen for the noise of the water! So Geoffrey was obliged to pull and they would say, "Ah, Bownas pulled again!"

When I was working with Geoffrey doing research for his book *'Japanese Journeys, Writings and Recollections'* we travelled to Japan in 2003. We went to the house, at least to see it from outside. It was difficult at first to find it, he hadn't been there since he left some 50 years before, and a lot had changed; but the house was still there. I said, "Well come on, let's knock on the door." A lady opened the door and she looked at Geoffrey and said, *"Bownas-sensei?"* and as it happened she was the grand-daughter of the owners, but she probably would not have remembered him as she was only a little girl then. But to see a *gaijin* outside her house, it could only be one *gaijin*, and that was Geoffrey!

We went inside the house, and saw where he lived. That part of the house was closed because one of the children who lived there was currently living in America, so they had covered the furniture. They often spoke about *Bownas-sensei*, because he lived there all that time he was in Kyoto. He cycled, and he used the Kyoto trams. It was a lovely story, and a lovely time to be there with him back in Fukakusa. There was also a *Fukakusa-ben* (dialect), and he always remembered on the tram, or on the train, the conductor or the ticket collector would come around at each station, and in the usual way they would bow nicely, and tell you the next station – *"Tsugi-wa Fukakusa desu!"*

A linguistic pioneer

Geoffrey pioneered many courses from the early 1950s. He was a linguist in both Chinese and Japanese, which is unusual, and the classics, and initiated the first Japanese degree course at Oxford in 1954.

He was first in Oxford when he was teaching Chinese and Japanese, and then in 1963 he was actually asked to set up Japanese Studies in Sheffield. Japanese, of course, was a rare language in universities in the early 1960s and, having set up Japanese at Oxford, Geoffrey took on the task of setting up Japanese at Sheffield with relish. This followed the recommendation that the study of the language should break the traditional mould and be linked to a subject like History or Economics; so Japanese studies combined with Law, Geography and Sociology, which was different from the existing Japanese studies at the time. There were four students in his first year!

Sheffield is where things took off, in terms of the oeuvre of Japanese studies in the UK and he was right at the pioneering point of that, to the extent that the Foreign Office moved their language tuition training for the diplomats to Sheffield. And as a result some of Geoffrey's pupils, such as Stephen Gomersall and Graham Fry, became British Ambassadors in Japan.

Promoting Japanese Studies in the UK

Geoffrey played a big part in lobbying the Japanese government, and the British government, to receive a grant to strengthen Japanese Studies, and to promote Japanese studies in the universities of the UK. In October 1973 he was very honoured to have been invited to Number 10 where the Prime Minister at the time, Sir Edward Heath, presented him with a cheque for one million U.S. dollars, which had been presented by the then Japanese Prime Minister Tanaka, a very nice gesture from his government.

The money was distributed, not just for Sheffield, but among all the universities in the UK that were promoting Japanese studies. After that, Edward Heath, every time they met, always asked him 'How's the Japanese studies project going?' so it formed quite a nice friendship; every time they met they remembered the event.

1964 Tokyo Olympic Games

Geoffrey went to Tokyo in August 1964 with the advanced party of the BBC's Olympic team as an interpreter. He arrived six weeks beforehand to help with the customs clearance, the venues, and all preparatory work. He involved one of his former students, Dr Brian Powell, who became an academic in his own right in Oxford, to assist John Snagge reporting on sailing and rowing and the language side. Geoffrey worked with David Coleman in the booth, and his story on watching the rehearsals for the preparation of the Opening Ceremony was told many times.

You have probably heard about the Five Rings; there were pilots doing their inter-loop with the Five Olympic Rings in the sky, but during the rehearsals there was always one who missed the loop! On the day the whole crowd was watching, maybe 75,000 at that time in the stadium, and when they had completed the loop, there was this, "Haaaah!" in the stadium, and then it went silent! Because everybody was watching, Geoffrey commented "Their necks were straight like cranes, strained up looking into the open air …"

When Ann Packer got to a semi-final and then went on to win a Gold in the Women's 800 metres, David Coleman was sitting next to Geoffrey and cried out in excitement! It was a bit different for me, as in 1964 I was a little girl living in Poland. We had a tiny television, and there were not many people who had one at that time, so all the neighbourhood gathered to watch it, and I remember vividly the Polish athletics, who won Gold for the 400 metres Women's 100 metres Relay. It just stuck in my mind, the euphoria and excitement of the entire street! So I wouldn't have known at that time about Ann Packer, but it's quite striking knowing Geoffrey was there! I wouldn't have heard Geoffrey's commentary about the craning necks in Poland, but he was very good with words, he was *par excellence* at describing things. I always think people should read his books for the English; he was very poetic in his descriptions.

As you know the Tokyo Olympics had the first *Shinkansen* (bullet train) that was launched, the monorail and the Yoyogi Olympic Park, these were three things the organisers did for the Olympics. There was a good clean up in Japan, they wanted to show the city in the best light, and there were all these preparations. There were lots of notices for people too, and I can quote you this: *"During the two weeks of the 18th Olympiad in Tokyo, Do not visit our bath-house in your underwear; Do not urinate in our neighbourhood streets; Do not allow your children to do the same; Maintain the fair name of our neighbourhood in the eyes of our Olympic visitors".*

When London hosted the Olympics in 2012 the Japanese Embassy put on a very nice photographic exhibition of the 1964 Tokyo Olympics in the foyer; it was free and open to the general public until the end of the Paralympics, on the 8th of September. It was very nice and I gave some of the memorabilia that Geoffrey had here about the 1964 Olympic Games and others who took part. There was also the Osaka Expo in 1970 and Geoffrey managed to get some on his Japanese students at Sheffield to man some of the stands, which was a great opportunity for them to actually practice the language.

Geoffrey was a keen sportsman and played cricket and rugby regularly. He was a right-arm fast bowler and played for his college and later as a member of a college staff – which is probably why he had trouble with his knees – playing too much cricket too late in life. His father taught him how to play cricket – as soon as he was able to hold a bat, he was out with him playing, so cricket was something he enjoyed. And he even got me interested! Probably he got fed up with me asking all sorts of daft questions, so he explained the rules to me and I got hooked!

Moving into the business world

Geoffrey was not ambitious for himself. He took early retirement and left Sheffield University in 1980. He was then one year from retirement but was ambitious for Japanese studies and learning about Japan in the UK, and that's when he moved more to the business side of it.

I think he was sought-after in the business world as he was a well-known expert on Japan at that time, and with such a variety of interests he was asked to advise on various topics. Once he went to Japan with the John Major government, because they wanted him there for very important negotiations. Geoffrey was the one who secured the Kansai Airport project for Watson Steel (a member of the AMEC group), so the steel you see there at Kansai airport comes from Bolton! It was Renzo Piano who designed that airport, although Kawasaki, who were very close to tender and to getting the project, were probably a bit scared about this new, modern design, so the bid was opened internationally, which was a good opportunity for the British to get it.

At that time Geoffrey was a consultant for AMEC, then a well-known construction company, no longer in business; he never had his own consultancy. Geoffrey told me that once they had secured the project, they had a big dinner party at the Imperial Hotel in Tokyo. Every time he went to Japan on business he would like to stay there as that was his favourite hotel, not only for the service, which was impeccable, but also for the location, very close to Tokyo station and Ginza; Hibiya Park is just across the road. He was a regular there to such an extent that the staff got to know him.

I once arrived with Geoffrey and we stayed at the Imperial Hotel, which for me was wonderful. The coach would pull up in front of the hotel, our luggage would be taken care of, and then when they saw him they were all bowing and saying with such an excitement, *"Bownas-sensei! Bownas-sensei!"* and carried his suitcase. When he checked in, a woman came and obviously remembered him from previous trips, like a VIP had arrived at the hotel! So when we were in the room, the phone rang, not only to welcome us but also to ask him, "As usual Mr Bownas, for your wake-up call, would you like the weather forecast?" They had on their records that this particular guest, when he wakes up, wants to know what the weather forecast is for that day. This had gone on for years and years, and had been remembered. There were lots of stories and of meetings held there, and some Japanese people told me that Geoffrey would give them English lessons in the bar over a gin and tonic! That was Geoffrey's idea to relax his students!

Overcoming trade barriers

There were quite a lot of trade barriers and difficulties with UK businesses trying to do business with Japan and although I don't know much about it, Geoffrey obviously was successful when he was conducting business, because he had this know-how. That's why he wanted to bring this awareness, to bring Japan to the UK, and that, I think, inspired, or prompted him, to do more on the business side of publications. He worked quite closely with Japan Air Lines and they produced the flyers and those little books *'The Do's and Don'ts in Japan'* which were very basic but also very important.

Geoffrey told me once that he would coach people who wanted to do business with Japan, and would coach them on the cultural differences, and how to do business in Japan with the Japanese, particularly if you wanted to be successful and sign the deal on the dotted line. There were plenty of business opportunities in the 1980s, and he told me that, having done all that, he would go beforehand to Japan to prepare the scene for them. Then the business people would arrive and the meeting would be arranged, having told them who sits where, the whole etiquette with *meishi* (business cards) and punctuality etc. – all terribly important in Japan at that time.

Perhaps things are a little bit different now, more westernised, but in the 1980s there were very strict rules and you observed those rules, particularly when the top boss would come to the meeting. There was one of those occasions when one of the top UK people came in late. The meeting had started, and Geoffrey was very concerned and thinking, "Where is this man?" He came in later and, in his rather arrogant manner, distributed his business cards as if he was dealing out the playing cards. At that moment the Kaicho (MD of the company) closed his papers, stood up without saying a word and left! The deal was over! It was that bad, and for Geoffrey obviously it was terribly embarrassing as it was seen as a gross misconduct and a lack of respect.

The turning point was after the Japanese economy plummeted. After the stock market crashed in late 1989, the Japanese had to change their ways to attract business. But some Japanese businesses are still very conservative to this day, but not to that extent I think. The seating plan, the hierarchy, the *nemawashi* (preparation) and *ringisho* (circulation); all that takes time to adapt. They were the canons and you couldn't change that. But if you want to be successful in Japan and you want to have that deal, you have to do things correctly. Japan was perhaps more conservative at that time, things are less formal now. I'm sure when we worked on the book published in 2003, *'Doing Business with the Japanese'*, things had changed a lot.

Geoffrey was commissioned to translate a book by a well-known Japanese philosopher, Watsuji Tetsuro, and his *Fudo*. He gave the title as *'Climate and Culture'*. This philosopher looks at the different climate of cultures, and how they work together and what makes people the way they are. He concentrated on the Monsoon zone, the Desert zone, and Meadows, which was greenery like here, and it was a very interesting book, well worth reading.

Working with Professor Bownas

The first project I worked on with Geoffrey was *'The Penguin Book of Japanese Verse'*. This was a new edition that introduced thirty new poems, *Shintaishi* poems. We worked with Anthony Thwaite, a poet. What an exciting project that was for me! To work with such prominent figures. The other one was *'Doing Business with the Japanese'*, when we had twenty contributors, with Geoffrey, David Powers and Dr Christopher Hood as co-editors. The book was dedicated to Sir Peter Parker, who very much inspired it, but who died suddenly before it was finished. I was the admin and manager of pulling it all together on the design side, and coordinating with all the contributors, plus I did a little bit myself on *'Notes on Japan – Sources of Support for British Businesses'*. The book sold well and was a one-stop guide to Japanese business practice, which Geoffrey felt was long overdue. Geoffrey's great skill was to pitch the book at the right level so that people could understand.

'Japanese Journeys: Writings and Recollections' was the most wonderful thing I could have done with Geoffrey, and I encouraged him because he did think of writing it and as other things were interfering he would put it off. I used to gently nudge

him to do it; and he would always say: "But who's going to read this?" It wasn't a memoir, or travelogue, it just talks about Japan spanning fifty years, from post-war abject poverty to this unimaginable prosperity, and his views. Again you can dip into various chapters, you don't need to follow it. He divides the book into part one and part two, and part two is perhaps more for academics, where he talks about Japanese aesthetics and poetry etc. The book is dedicated to Professor Kaizuka Shigeki, his *sensei* at Kyoto University. It was such a privilege to be working with him.

Sometimes it was quite frustrating for me because Geoffrey was very pedantic and everything had to be right, to the extent that I told him that to do it he had to learn how to use the computer, because typewriters were no longer in use! We worked well as a team – 'Cook-Bownas team' he would call us. I did quite a lot of research as I was more IT orientated. Hence our trip together to Japan in 2003, to find out more, go to where he used to live, and meet up with various people .The book came out in 2005.

Friendships

Geoffrey's life was a full one and he was admired and loved by very many people across the generation divide. He made many friends and on his various trips to Japan he would always try to see at least some of them. He kept in touch with business associates who were seconded to the UK, and when they left for Japan the number of Christmas cards received showed how much he was respected and remembered right to his last Christmas in 2010.

Geoffrey was a very modest man and when I tried to tell other people that he's a Professor of Japanese studies, his reaction would be, "Shush!"; he didn't want to say anything, so it was me who would say something. He had rare qualities – enthusiasm and enthusing others, endless energy, modesty and instant likeability.

Geoffrey made many friends in Japan over the years, and a lot of his friends, when they would go out together, would go to sushi bars, or somewhere where they would want to speak Japanese. But there was one particular family, the Uyeno family, to whom he actually dedicated his *"Japanese Journeys"* ; he had known them since 1963 when he was still in Oxford. The father was in the shipping business, and they were very helpful to Geoffrey with the customs clearance for the Olympic Games. He helped one of the sons get into Oxford, and now I have met, at the Memorial Lecture for Geoffrey in 2011 in Oxford, a third generation member of the family studying at the Nissan Institute. With the Uyeno family in particular, this link now spans over three generations.

I was introduced to the Uyeno family in Kamakura, where they had a beautiful house with a tea house and a big garden, on our earlier visits to Japan. Geoffrey had kept in touch with them over the years. They did business together, or Geoffrey helped to introduce business for them, advised them, and vice versa and they had created a wonderful bond. He knew he could always call on this old friendship. And now I am happy to continue that link and friendship and I'm truly grateful to Geoffrey for giving me that.

A shared love of Japan

My own contact with Japan goes back to when I was fifteen, that's quite a long time ago. I happened to have a Japanese pen-pal when I was still living in Poland. I wish I had kept her letters now, as she told me all about Japan; she would send me little things, about the language, and little gifts. We were both fifteen at that time, and our friendship actually survived and I went to Japan for the first time in 1985 to meet her. I was living in the Middle East at the time, she met me at the bus terminal in Tokyo and the first thing she asked me was, "How do I pronounce your name?" because obviously she had only seen it written! She lived in a tiny apartment outside Tokyo in Hiyoshi, which was near the Keio University campus. I was there for about four weeks, and got completely bowled over. I went all over Kanto and Kansai with her. We were out almost every day, but because she worked, I also did things by myself. What I wanted was an address in Japanese, in case I got lost, as I could not speak anything, other than 'Thank you' I suppose, and that was it. I also experienced my first earthquake there!

I got more involved with Japan when I worked for the Daiwa Foundation, and certainly with Geoffrey it was more than anything else. Now I'm really grateful that he kind of instilled in me that love for Japan. And that helped in our relationship too, we formed a good understanding of Japan, and he was a very wise and knowledgeable person; all his stories I could listen to forever. Knowing Geoffrey and being with him in Japan obviously strengthened my love for Japan, and it's just something you can't describe in words. It gets into you when the plane lands at Narita or Haneda airport; there is something so special for me about Japan.

Japan meant a lot to Geoffrey and as for his favourite place, he talked about the "Kyoto effect". In his poetry he talks about Japanese aesthetics, and for him the *sounds* of Japan were very important. The sound of the whistle of the JR train, the sound of the *tofu* sellers, the *shakuhachi*, the *koto*, or the *shamisen* musical instruments, also the cicadas, the *semi* – he always talked about the summer *semi*, or the sound of water. In Kyoto in those days when it was very hot and there was no air conditioning, the *mizu no oto*, the sound of water would have this cooling effect. So there were all these different sounds, and that stayed with him. Even during the last trip, he would be just happy to sit, and watch, and listen, the visual and the aural for him were very important. But to summarise, for him, when the train would pull in to Kyoto station, he would say *"Tadaima!"* and to him that was home. I always knew that when Geoffrey was there, his eyes were lit up. He would say, "You know, you could never be upset or unhappy in Japan".

Sometimes he said that if he got old and no longer of use to anybody, "I'll go to Japan and die there". I wondered how it would have been, with what happened in Tohoku in March 2011, if he had still been alive. I know he would have been terribly upset and devastated, but still having a lot of positive thoughts about Japan, that Japan would rebuild herself; he always had that view about Japan.

An invaluable legacy

Geoffrey has made important contributions to Japanese studies, but in my view the most important thing is that he fostered the knowledge of Japan in so many ways, not just as a scholar, but also in the business context. He was a person of many parts, and the importance of linguistics and cultural skills in an economic context, in my view, was his most important contribution.

As for the future – a couple of his former pupils took the lead in establishing a lasting memory of Geoffrey. It was their way of saying *Thank You* for his inspiration and for helping them so much and enthusing them about Japan. Most of them went on to have wonderful careers involving Japan; and they felt there was a 'payback', to give something back to him for what he's done. Next year Sheffield University will celebrate the fiftieth anniversary of setting up Japanese studies in Sheffield, and they felt following his death, there should be something in his name; so The Geoffrey Bownas Memorial Fund has been established in Sheffield, for the fellowships, for Post-Doctorate and Fellowship studies, hopefully also for a permanent Chair. So there is going to be a big opening next year, and they are very ambitious and hope to raise a significant amount of money to secure a permanent Chair. So I'm obviously involved with that.

I know he left a legacy, we all know that. Although he had never spoken about it, I think he knew that people would be reading his books for years to come. One of his translations, called '*Kappa*', is used at universities as a translation tool for the undergraduates studying Japanese. It's doing very well...

Geoffrey Bownas was an extraordinary man and I am very happy to have been part of his life. Together we created a true partnership at a time when for most people the chance for that might have been lost.

SIR GEOFFREY BOWNAS
IN HIS OWN WORDS

When Sir Geoffrey introduced himself to a Japanese audience he would often use a play on words:

"Now, to begin, my name is Bownas. 'Bownas' (pron. 'bonus') is a good name, isn't it?" Once I say it, for Japanese people it's an unforgettable name!"

Thoughts about Japan:

"Japan's a place where everything is happening. It's an exciting place, it's always on the move, never still, always probing to find new aspects of living, of life, of culture. And if you just step on that moving vehicle, you'll never stop, and you'll love being moved".

In 1970 Professor Bownas co-edited the edition of '*New Writing in Japan*' for Penguin Books with the Japanese author Yukio Mishima:

"During the summer of that year we met almost every day to move the book forward. In November of that year Mishima killed himself. Afterwards I recollected that he'd said in a very quiet and calm voice, "Japan's culture faces a greater threat now than ever before." He was just uneasy that this new affluence would drive into the background all the cultural, the old traditional cultural canons and values of Japan".

"But I don't think Mishima's anxiety was justified. Foreign observers have always been so ready to talk about Japan relinquishing its values, and writing off Japan, not just economically or in terms of economic development, but also in terms of preserving Japanese culture. I think, there was no reason to be so afraid, or any reason to be anxious today..... Looking out of the hotel window, there it was – lively, people walking smartly, people smiling – there's that kind of enlivening feel about this city, Tokyo".

SIR GEOFFREY BOWNAS CBE

Sino-Japanese Scholar and Linguist, Founder of the Centre of Japanese Studies at Sheffield

1923	Born in Yorkshire, England
1942-3	Joined the army; Catterick military parade ground last 'volunteer' for learning Japanese language
1945	After demob, returned to Oxford, completed Classics at Queen's College with first class degree, went to Aberystwyth as classics lecturer
1948	Returned to Oxford for second degree in Chinese studies
1952-54	Two years in Japan working with Sinologist Prof Kaizuka Shigeki; later translated his book on Confucius into English
1954	Appointed lecturer in Chinese & Japanese at Oxford, the first to hold such a post
1963	Established Oxford's first full honours degree in Japanese
1964	Translator for BBC team at Tokyo Olympics; published *Penguin Book of Japanese Verse* (second edition 1998)
1965	Moved to Sheffield as first Professor of Japanese and as first Director of its Centre of Japanese Studies, pioneering a new type of degree that combined equal training in history, social science and language studies
1974	Published *Business in Japan*, co-edited with Paul Norbury; did consultancy for car industry and wrote for the *Financial Times* on Japanese business practice
1980	Took early retirement to work independently; worked as a consultant to many businesses and educational organisations
1990-91	Conducted business ventures with UK and Japan; wrote *Japan and the New Europe*, a special report for the Economist Intelligence Unit

2003   Published *Doing Business with the Japanese*; consulted on JET scheme and Sir Peter Parker awards

2005   Elected Vice President of the Chartered Institute of Linguists, promoting language teaching in Japanese

2009   *Penguin Book of Japanese Verse* (3rd edition) published by the Penguin Classics series; married Wiesia Cook

2011   Died February 17th in London

HONOURS

1999   Awarded Order of Sacred Treasure with Sun's Rays by the Japanese government

2003   Conferred CBE (Commander of the Order of the British Empire) in recognition of a lifetime's contribution to education, scholarship and the improvement of Anglo-Japanese relations in commercial and cultural spheres

WIESIA COOK-BOWNAS
Widow of SIR GEOFFREY BOWNAS

Born in Poland

Had first encounter with Japan at the age of 15 when living in Poland.

1985	First went to Japan, spent one month travelling around with Japanese pen-friend
1993	Joined Daiwa Anglo-Japanese Foundation as a programme administrator where she met Geoffrey Bownas in 1994
2002	Left Daiwa to work on the Japan Business Projects, and Direct Image/Hen Di Creative project
2000s	Worked on many books with Geoffrey, including *Penguin Book of Japanese Verse (2nd Edition in 1998 and the Penguin Classic in 2009), Doing Business with the Japanese,* and *Japanese Journeys, Writings and Recollections*
	Visited Japan regularly since 1985 independently and also travelled as Geoffrey's companion.
2009	Wiesia and Geoffrey were married
2011	Wiesia continued to work on all projects with Geoffrey until his death in 2011
2013	The Geoffrey Bownas Memorial Fund was established at Sheffield University to mark the 50th Anniversary of the Centre of Japanese Studies
2015	Continues to work in promoting Anglo-Japanese organisations, supporting The Geoffrey Bownas Memorial Fund at Sheffield University, and including Poland-Japan-UK international education links

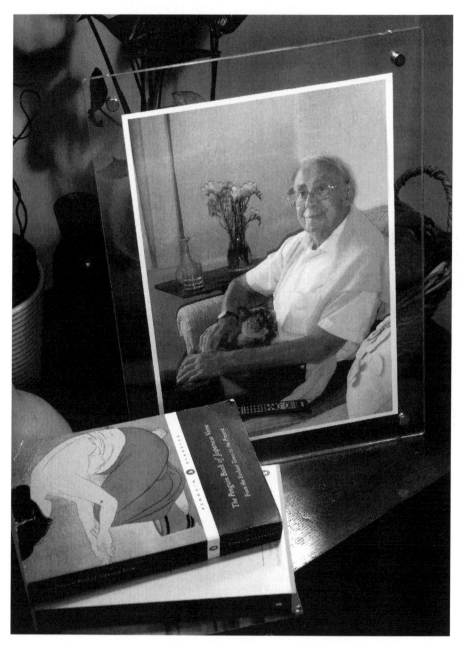

Professor Bownas's publications on Japanese Verse

JOJI HIROTA

INTERNATIONAL PERCUSSIONIST AND MUSICAL DIRECTOR

"Fundamentally I'm Japanese, yes, but more a global musician too. Because I'm using pure Japanese folk song melody, but supported with so many different kinds of beautiful western harmonies and the orchestral strings.

"Always there were all those people I worked with who helped my brain to open! Inspired, yes, so my brain is wider than before."

Joji Hirota

Early musical influences

I was born in Hokkaido and my first musical influence was my father. He loved singing Japanese folk songs, and playing *shakuhachi* (Japanese flute). He would sing and play *shakuhachi* mostly every night. So naturally I got something from him, Japanese songs – even though I wasn't very keen on it at that time.

I started percussion when I was eleven. I was always interested in it from when I was in school in a drum & pipe group. So from the age of eleven, my focus has always been on my music.

Studying at Kyoto University of Arts

I had a senior friend, a professional percussionist, in the Kyoto Municipal Symphony Orchestra, and he inspired me to go to music college. He first introduced me to a professor in Osaka Music College, and I eventually went to Kyoto University of Arts to study music.

Travelling to Europe with the Japanese Red Buddha Theatre

Stomu Yamashita worked in the same college that I went to in Kyoto. He had already made a big success in America as a contemporary percussionist, and he came back to Kyoto when I was there. He had an invitation to go to Avignon in France, for their annual festival, and his idea was that instead of doing a solo performance, he wanted to have more collaboration – we used to call it 'total art'. You know: the lighting, the design, the music, the art, the whole staging of the production. He asked me to do some musical collaboration. He had already called up the lighting designer, the artists and musicians for the events in France starting with Paris. So that was my first time in Europe, the first time out of the country really. And language? Well, I had just a little bit of English and French. All Japanese have a little bit of English!

We rehearsed in Paris at the theatre of the famous designer Pierre Cardin. It was very beautiful and I did a lot of walking around the city, enjoying the smells of Gitanes and coffee, the coffee shops, *café au lait!* And using their Metro, underground. I was just over twenty, and it was a very, very exciting time for me.

I'm not sure why it was called *The Red Buddha Theatre*. Red is one of the original colours, a colour of nature, and Buddhism is one of our main philosophies, so maybe Stomu Yamashita wanted to fit these things together, and maybe he wanted to create some stage production between nature and philosophy – combining eastern philosophy in the 1970s, a kind of 'free art', with Buddhist philosophy, and of Hiroshima, in modern times. So using artists in modern times to create a new kind of Japanese history and philosophy, and giving people the new feeling of 'after the War and Future' things. It was a very, very big success.

We toured all over the world for two and a half years, including Europe and the UK, and the USA: New York, San Francisco, Los Angeles.

London: the Roundhouse and Sadler's Wells

We came to London, which was very exciting, a very beautiful place, and we had a long run at the Roundhouse and the Piccadilly Theatre. In fact before we did the Roundhouse we had a short performance time at the ICA (Institute of Contemporary Arts), then we went back to Paris, then came back again to do the Roundhouse for a longer period, and had another big success.

My staying in London was accidental really, I didn't choose it! The manager was English, so he arranged for us to stay there and all the activities were based in London. That's how it started. During my time with Yamashita and the Red Buddha Theatre I did only one production. They did maybe two more productions with the same company, but I did only one, mainly percussion, and singing.

Then I worked on Lindsay Kemp's *Onnagata* at Sadler's Wells. I did three productions within it: one of Jean Genet's *Flowers*, and Oscar Wilde's *Salome*. *Onnagata* received a Time Out Award for the Lindsay Kemp production. I worked closely with Lindsay on the music, as musical director and composer, and talked to him about the inspiration for that. His father was a sailor, and he travelled all over the world including Japan, and when Lindsay was really young, his father would talk about Japan, and bring back souvenirs. So Lindsay had a lot of admiration for Japanese things, and wanted to express a reflection of his life, through this project, *Onnagata*. Of course he used his ideas, he's a fantastic artist, and knows all about music. Lindsay used classical music, Japanese music, jazz, and lots of different music – including my influence of Japanese music – so he was very creative.

Wider musical influences

Towards the end of the 1980s I went to see my Taiko Master in Hokkaido, in Nobori Betsu. His name was Maestro Itto Ohba and his son was Kazuoki Ohba. His Taiko group was called *Hokkai-Daiko* Group, and I studied the fundamental Taiko technique, and that was my Taiko drumming foundation. Sadly they both died, but their message was: *"You should create your own music, don't just copy my music; use my technique as a foundation, but you must find a new Taiko music for your audience, and use your own way to present Taiko music."* So that's what I'm doing.

Percussion was always my basic instrument. For example in the Lindsay Kemp production I had a very big set with lots of drums, lots of bells, a gong, and sometimes I had to play piano and other instruments. That made me develop my performing technique and my musical ideas, which was very good.

Lindsay Kemp was a very important person in my development, as was everybody really; no one is really the 'best'. But I listened to all kinds of music over here: classical music, Richard Strauss, Bela Bartok, John McLoughlin, and to a lot of English composers like Edward Elgar and Vaughan Williams; they were an inspiration to me, very much so.

Most recently what has influenced me in my music are really the Japanese folk songs, and in Western music it's Elgar – I love Elgar – and Debussy, Ravel, the beautiful melody and harmony of the Romantics. Actually Taiko drumming is more like jazz, I could do that, take it in that direction, but I have both sides; the other side is more beautiful, harmonious, melodic, passionate. I'm speaking of a really sensitive, passion in things; also I really love spiritual music too. So I have two opposites: one is really dynamic and powerful music, the other is really sensitive, beautiful and colourful. My Taiko setting is very dynamic, with a huge and powerful Taiko drum, but also using bells and chimes.

WOMAD

In the 1980s and 1990s, I met Guo Yue (Chinese flautist) and Pol Brennan (formerly of Clannad) at Peter Gabriel's WOMAD festivals, and we worked together on *Trisan.* They were quite specific influences, being Chinese and Irish. I got such a big influence meeting so many artists from all over the world, it made my mind very open. Peter Gabriel established world music to be more popular.

I played at so many WOMAD festivals. I don't do very much now, but I did most of them then, every year, every month, I even went to South Korea. I received a call from WOMAD so I went from London to perform Japanese Taiko drumming in South Korea! This was somewhere in the central Korean peninsula, a town called Chugiu – it was a cultural centre town, all culture started in this town which was chosen for its heritage. So I got some influence from South Korean music, because we had a lot of South Korean artists there, musicians, dancers, it was really nice. Sometimes farmers came and danced. The origins of Japanese music are close there, as we have influences from Korea and *Gagaku* (Japanese court music) comes from Korea.

The Royal Shakespeare Company

The Royal Shakespeare Company used my sounds for the production of *Macbeth.* It was at their Swan Theatre in Stratford-Upon-Avon, and I had a big set-up with my instruments and things, like a really deep Taiko drum sound, or some large gong sound, and other very delicate bell sounds. They liked their music to be used like this, with really strange sound effects, and they thought that my sounds were really effective. The opening sequence had a huge thunder sound, and I had to use a big metal sound sheet and gong, and a big Taiko drum, to create a huge storm effect and people were really surprised! "What's going on?" they said!

Even when I went to Japan, even when I went to Tokyo to perform *Macbeth* with the RSC, people in Japan said, "Why are you doing Taiko drumming here? Is it because you're performing in Tokyo?" No, no, I said, I use this Taiko when we perform in England or America, everywhere!

So they are used to musical effects. I think the RSC is very creative. Gregory Doran was the Director, and he's the Artistic Director at the RSC now. They were very good to work with, the young English actors were so talented. Also I worked with Anthony Sher, who played Macbeth. He loved my sound, and we got on very well, and Harriet Waters was his Lady Macbeth. I also worked with Patrick Stewart in another production, *Anthony & Cleopatra*, which I did for the RSC. I did four productions for them, and there was another project for actors and local children. I'm still doing occasional workshops for actors and children – they love doing Taiko drumming!

As to staging, it's important to create a whole thing, not just the music itself. I think that because I worked a lot with Lindsay Kemp and the RSC, so I think stage work is very important. But I'm a musician, so I concentrate more on the music.

The London Metropolitan Orchestra

When I worked with the Metropolitan London Orchestra in 1999 for the first time there were only five members, and I recorded the first album called *Gate* with them. That one I did because my father died, and I wanted to dedicate some music to him. Actually, I wanted to play *Eishi oiwake* - one of his favourite songs that he sang every night, but I couldn't sing – it's one of the most difficult songs to sing! I wanted to play it my way, somehow, and to commemorate him. That's where it started, arranging string instruments for Japanese folk songs. Then it developed more and more. But this project is always about more personal things. My mother was a modern radio choir singer, so I had a kind of Western musical influence from her. So I did my own arrangement for one of the Japanese lullabies she sang to me when I was a child.

My recent collaboration with the London Metropolitan Orchestra for *Beyond a Requiem* was very different, because it was all my arrangements for Japanese music, especially Japanese folk music; I arranged the orchestration. I was performing, playing the *shakuhachi*, singing and doing some drumming, and all the composing, so this was really different.

2011 Earthquake & Tsunami

The Tsunami affected all Japanese people; that's why I did the music for that. From 1999 I always did some fusions of Japanese folk and other songs. After the Tsunami I arranged the folk music of the three prefectures which were heavily affected. I arranged their folk songs, specifically, because I thought their folk music had such a strong message, about life, about people's working things, people's relationships, love, nature, everything. There is such a strong message, and that's why I thought, "My God, this looks so realistic, it's exactly what they have to listen to, they have to share their loss". So I did *Beyond a Requiem* for them.

Everything, they lost everything. But what they need now is some special help, and music is very good, especially for them to have their own music, I think it's very effective for them. If it is haunting, and heart-felt, it is because the arrangement is for the people, now, for them. That's why I'm not just arranging or presenting Japanese folk songs, I'm presenting *their* feelings and it's a present for *them*, to help them. That's why there's a special musical arrangement, the arrangement is completely different.

I did concerts including schools in Japan in 2012 and 2013, for the Tohoku region in the three prefectures including Tohoku, Hokkaido and Tokyo with the London Metropolitan Orchestra and Japanese Orchestra.

There is a new CD called *Japanese Folk Songs II* which came out in June 2013 and includes these folk songs. In the booklet I explain why I did the arrangements as it's focusing on the Tohoku region folk songs. Also there are many English people who are very sympathetic and supportive and they went to help the Tsunami victims. So all the Japanese people, they really wanted to say "Thank you", from here as well.

Japanese or Global?

Fundamentally I think of myself as Japanese, but a global musician too. For example I'm using pure Japanese folk song melody, but supported with so many different kinds of beautiful Western harmonies and strings. So fundamentally Japanese, but I think global too. All those people I have worked with helped my brain to open! They inspired me, so my brain is wider than before. I'm very Japanese now, with these beautiful Japanese folk songs. I tried as much as possible to keep to the original, my music is always very original, melody-wise, but wide; if you listen to it, it's beautiful. Put together with Western strings and harmonies, it's supporting that original song, but also making it more accessible to other people, I hope.

I've produced many albums, and all of them had a special reason, but I don't have a favourite. I played with the Kodo Drummers in Bruges with Guo Yue (flautist) and we played one song together that was good. So Taiko became very popular, and is still growing; now there are many groups in the UK and Europe.

Looking to the future

I'm planning to have a Taiko drumming *Dojo,* a workshop and study centre for the further development of Japanese Taiko drumming activities and also for educational purposes. I need a good space in London, and it would have to be completely soundproofed!

Promoting Japanese culture, or any cultural activities, is always related to the economy, it's a fundamental thing. But our culture is the foundation for everything. That's why South Korea is a big success, because about twenty years ago the government there promoted all their own, original Korean culture first. That's why Koreans always work, always do business, and it's very important to have a cultural base.

I don't know if I'd ever go back to Japan to live. Recently I've been going a lot to Japan, and I like Japan very much, of course. There's good food, nice people, the countryside and scenery is especially beautiful. I went to a lake, to a Japanese *onsen* (spa) with good food, beautiful rice! Well, London is my life and working base, and Japan is my *furusato,* spiritual base.

JOJI HIROTA

International Percussionist and Musical Director, Founder of the First London Taiko Drummers Group

Born in Otaru Hokkaido, northern Japan

Started percussion at the age of 11 at school in a drum and pipe group

Studied at Kyoto University of Arts Music Department

1970s Toured with the Red Buddha Theatre in France at Avignon Music Festival, then in Europe, the USA, New York and San Francisco, and finally came to the Round House and The West End in London

1980s Formed *Taiko* Drumming group Joji Hirota London Taiko Drummers; performed in UK (opening act for Live Earth at Wembley Stadium etc) USA, Europe, Middle East, Asia and Japan, including Japan Foundation's governmental projects

1990s Worked with Lindsay Kemp Co, doing dance productions for *Onnagata,* Jean Genet's *Flowers* and Oscar Wilde's *Salome* at Sadler's Wells London, toured worldwide

Performed at Peter Gabriel's WOMAD festivals worldwide (Hanover Expo etc), also met and worked with Chinese flautist Guo Yue and Irish musician Pol Brennan, produced album *Trisan*

Worked with the Royal Shakespeare Company for music and sound on productions of *Macbeth, Julius Caesar, Anthony and Cleopatra* and others

1999 Started working with the London Metropolitan Orchestra and produced the album *The Gate,* subsequent collaboration lasted into 2000s; toured in Japan with them several times

2000s Continued touring with Taiko group, performing large collaborative music events, festivals, and BBC TV appearance; also charitable teaching for schools and children

2011   Tohoku earthquake and tsunami hit northern Japan in March; Joji responds by creating *Beyond the Requiem* supporting concerts based on his arrangements of Tohoku folk songs. CD album *Japanese Folk Songs II* released 2013

2014   Performed at the prestigious Kiyoi Hall in Tokyo

2015   Continues to write and arrange music producing solo albums, appearing on TV with international musicians and touring with *Beyond the Requiem*

AWARDS

1990   Lindsay Kemp Group won *Time Out* Award for Best Dance Company with Joji as composer and musical director

1993   *Trisan* received Tower Records' Best Contemporary Music album in New York

2003   Awarded Ambassador's Commendation Award by Japanese Embassy in UK in recognition of his musical contribution to the world throughout his 30-year career

2007   Newsweek voted Joji in *Top 100 Japanese Respected in the World*

Joji Hirota performing with his female Taiko Group, 2013

ROBERT KETCHELL

GARDEN DESIGNER AND AUTHOR, CO-FOUNDER OF THE JAPANESE GARDEN SOCIETY

"To observe the inner form and structure of the garden you're much more concerned with the rock arrangement, the 'ishigumi' that is the skeleton of the garden.

"And that's why in Japan they place much more emphasis on rock arrangements. A measure of a gardener is how well he arranges his stones, not necessarily how well he arranges the planting."

Robert Ketchell

First interest in gardening, and Japanese gardens

My first contact with Japan was probably in England: in fact, at Tatton Park, because my earliest memory of a Japanese garden was being taken there with my mother. We lived in Cheshire, and I would have been in my early teens; I was already interested in gardening. It's something I've always done.

My father was also interested in gardening. I don't think he would have called himself a gardener, but he liked gardening, and I'd always wanted to work outdoors, to work with my hands. That didn't really please him too much!

When I was studying horticulture at Askham Bryan College in Yorkshire I came across books on Japanese gardens in the library, and that really awoke my interest. I also had a very longstanding interest in Buddhism, and in Chinese culture as well, so it was a kind of coming together of various tributaries, really.

After I'd graduated from Askham Bryan College I came down to live in London, and it was during that time I became more interested in Japanese gardens and this kind of Eastern culture. It became more prominent in my life in many ways.

An 'accidental' apprenticeship in Kyoto

In 1980 I went to Japan for the first time. I was travelling overland to India, doing the path of Buddhism from Japan back to its source in reverse, but I never got any further than Japan! I just absolutely fell in love with the place. It was the most extraordinary time that I've ever known in my life. Literally within a few weeks of arriving in Japan I had a job, and I got to meet the professor of landscape architecture at Kyoto University, who invited me to become a research student, which sorted out my visa, because I'd just arrived there with a tourist visa. I hadn't planned on staying in Japan at all; in the end I stayed for about three and a half years.

About two weeks after I arrived in Japan, I literally bumped into somebody in the street in Kyoto. I turned around and apologised in English, and he said, "Oh, you speak English!" and it turned out he was running a small English language school and was looking for native speakers. So I had coffee with him and kept saying that I'd never taught anybody, I didn't know how to teach, and he said, "It's not a problem, they're all eight years old, they don't speak English anyway!" The bait that I went for was that he said, "If you come and teach for me, I'll introduce you to a very famous gardener in Kyoto." So I thought, "That's fine."

So I went along to meet this famous Japanese gardener. This was Mr Kobayashi, who owned a large landscaping company of Kyoto gardeners, which had been going for about four or five generations. A Japanese person I knew a little translated, because I couldn't speak any Japanese at all. We had a very interesting conversation and at the end of an hour or so he turned to me, and through the translator, asked, "When do you want to start?" So I said, "Start what?" Then the translator said to me, "Mr Kobayashi (Susumu) is offering for you to become an apprentice," so I said "Pardon?" and I was just floored. I thought, well, maybe for a couple of weeks, it would be an interesting experience, so I said "Yes, okay.". I wasn't going to get paid, it was just for the experience. And that's how I became an 'accidental' apprentice.

At the same time I met the professor of landscape architecture at Kyoto University, Professor Nakamura. He was writing a book about Capability Brown, so he was interested to meet an English gardener who, of course, must know all about Capability Brown, as you do! That gave me access to the university, the library and the professors there. And, because I was officially a research student, I got a study visa. I'd arrived there with a 90-day tourist visa, thinking I'd only stay a few weeks, but now all I needed was a letter from the professor once a year and I would get my visa renewed. Without any effort or plan, everything just fell into place. It was really quite bizarre!

'It takes ten years to make a gardener'

The whole business of being an apprentice in Japan is so different to what we expect in the West. As an apprentice you just kind of devote your life to the work, and you do what you're told. It wasn't a formal programme of education in any sense.

I saw this man as being my teacher, so I expected to be taught, but you don't get that, and that caused a lot of tension in the beginning for me. I didn't know what to expect; I couldn't speak the language, the people I was working with didn't really speak very much English, and Kobayashi-san didn't speak any English at all. We worked practically every day, seven days a week. I was going to university one day a week, which they thought odd. Kobayashi-san would often ask me, "Why do you go to university?"

The first few months I was there, they were building a large, very formal, European-style rose garden in the Botanic Gardens in Kyoto, and that's where I was working all the while. That was not what I wanted to be doing at all and it came to the point where I said I was going to leave, because I'd met another gardener, through a priest I knew at Daitoku-ji temple. This gardener worked with only four or five people, and he said "We work at this temple, and that temple", which was much more what I'd wanted, to have that kind of experience, not planting roses to create an English garden!

This became a big conflict in my mind, and I asked a friend – a priest – for advice and he told me that as an apprentice you give up everything. And I remember saying to him, "I'm only here for a few months, I don't have the time, I want to go round and get more experience of gardeners." I knew that by saying I wanted to resign I was cutting into the norms of social etiquette, but with the help of the priest I concocted a resignation speech, in Japanese, which I learnt by heart. And then I asked to see Kobayashi-san, and I just launched into this little speech. I got about three-quarters of the way through, and saw that his face was ashen, I mean he was so angry you wouldn't believe. And this long reply came back, which I couldn't understand, and he turned round and stormed off. I was left standing there in the middle of the Botanic garden, wondering what had just happened.

The next day I went to work again, just to see what was happening, and nobody spoke to me. There was something like 22 or 25 apprentices, and obviously word had got round. For a week I kept turning up to work because I didn't know what else to do! Then, I remember very clearly, I was in the Botanic garden and it was lunchtime, and I was sitting on my own, and Kobayashi-san came over. His nickname was '*Kumo*', the 'Bear', because he was a very well-built man. I saw him walking over to me and I knew that this was going to be the moment when the situation would be resolved, though I still didn't have any idea as to what the situation was, exactly, between us. He sat next to me, and, in English, he said, "I'm going to teach you about Japanese gardens." That was the only time he ever spoke to me in English.

From then onwards we had the most fantastic relationship. I think it was a kind of breakthrough, because he realised that I was serious about learning. I think there had always been an element of doubt in his mind, because I was seen as an apprentice. I didn't understand this at the time, but as an apprentice you are expected to give up your life to your teacher and to go through a process of actually proving that you are worthy of being taught. Afterwards I began to realise that everybody, the other apprentices who came, went through a similar process. It's like 'your will is tested, your body is tested, and if you can cope with that, then you are accepted, then we'll start teaching you! '

After that point, there was a palpable change in the whole relationship, and we became very close, and he became like a father-figure to me.

I had stepped into a very traditional world, about which I had no idea, not a clue. I probably knew more about China and Chinese culture than Japan at that time, really. Being an apprentice opened up the possibility to be able to learn. What I'd learnt was that your teacher doesn't teach you anything, but he gives you the opportunity to learn, and to absorb, through an osmotic process. It's not like in the West where, in a teaching situation, you give people information or you dig into your own experience to try to explain something. In Japan I found it was more a question of you being put into a situation where you are allowed to learn, allowed to absorb that information; more than information, you are allowed to absorb that experience. That's why an apprenticeship for a gardener takes ten years and, as Kobayashi-san said to me, "Even after ten years, some people will be gardeners, and some people won't."

But I didn't finish my apprenticeship! I came back from Japan after three and a half years. I had married an English girl in Japan, and she was pregnant with our daughter and didn't want to have the baby in Japan. Also, her mum was dying of cancer so, although I was really settled and loving it in Japan, it was what we had to do.

So we moved back to Cheshire, where Lauren, our daughter, was born, and I set up a landscaping business and realised I had to start all over again. Although my time in Japan was a very profound experience, in some respects I'd just been pointed in a certain direction and I feel to this day that I'm still learning my craft. I'm still finding my way with it all, and trying to find a way of how to re-interpret the Japanese garden tradition in a different culture. Because I never wanted to just replicate what I've seen and experienced in Kyoto; that doesn't seem to me to be the point.

But this was really the beginning of this process, 'How do I express some of these ideas?' This is still not particularly well defined in my mind – the process of discovery is still going on!

The elements of a Japanese garden

What are the important elements in a Japanese garden, as opposed to a Western garden? I think it has a lot to do with the way space is perceived, and also there's a very strong element of the Japanese garden which has been influenced by Chinese landscape painting; the connection between painting and gardens is very strong.

One of the things that you learn from looking at the paintings is that the garden is a composition, and seeing the garden as a composition – and how that's put together – is something very different to a Western garden. In terms of observing inner form and structure, with a Western garden you're much more concerned with its outward appearance, whereas with a Japanese garden you're very much concerned with the skeleton. Kobayashi-san used to talk about planting being the 'flesh on the bones', whereas, for example, the rock arrangement, the *ishigumi*, is the skeleton. And that's why in Japan they place much more emphasis on rock arrangements. A measure of a gardener is how well he arranges his stones, not necessarily how well he arranges the planting.

Because the rocks are such an important and intrinsic part of the garden, when I do a garden the rocks have the same kind of symbolic form. The symbolic association is something which is applied by the creator of the garden by or through the intention of what you are trying to do. This intention can exist, but it doesn't necessarily have to.

All the materials that go into a Japanese garden are seen as being patterns of energy, and that's very much true of rocks as well. Plants are obviously forms of energy because you can see a plant change from one season to the next, you can see how it responds to light, and the conditions. A rock is much more subtle, because the time scale inherent within a rock is almost beyond comprehension. But a rock also contains a pattern of energy, and that's what you're actually arranging. We call it 'a rock', we might call it 'a pine tree', 'an azalea', we might call it 'gravel', we might call it 'water', they're all individual elements, but fundamentally they're all expressions of energy. And that's the material that you're working with when you're creating a Japanese garden. You're seeing beyond it being a rock, you're seeing beyond it being a pine tree; it IS a pine tree, it IS a rock, but also it's a pattern of energy, a movement, a flow of energy. And then the viewer, the person who comes in to see that garden, introduces another aspect, becomes a participant in that energy pattern. That's part of the way of seeing that you learn from looking at Japanese gardens, and being there was really revelatory.

The garden creator

One key aspect in creating a garden is what the garden creator carries within themselves. It's not necessarily that you have to find a rock in the shape of a dragon, for example, to represent the energy of a dragon in a rock. But you can create a stone arrangement in the form that represents a dragon and it might be something quite subtle. So the intention of the garden creator is really important, because what you carry as your intention comes out in the work. It's one thing that I'm always very keen to stress with people when I work with them, that whatever they bring to the work will come out. In a subtle form, but a form that does impact on the viewer. So if you want someone to have a harmonious experience you've got to carry that harmony, or intention of harmony, within yourself, not just in the way you put the various elements in the garden together.

While part of the training of a gardener is obviously to do with technique, how you arrange rocks, how you put the plants together, etc., an equally important part of the process is a kind of training of your own spirit. It's like Zen meditation, which I practice, in that there's no actual division. We talk about an interiorisation, or an exteriorisation, but that's just a relative concept. There isn't actually a separation between the two. Which is why your teacher doesn't teach you. Kobayashi-san used to say to me, "I don't understand why you go to the university," He said, "I'm sixty – whatever it was – years old, I'm only starting to learn this sort of stuff, about the history and all the rest of it" which wasn't actually true, he knew an awful lot about that kind of thing. But to him it was 'absorb it through your hands', 'absorb it through your body' and not have this kind of split. I used to ask him questions all the time, "Why are we doing this?"; "Who was Soami?"; "Who built Ginkakuji temple?"; "What ideas were they trying to express?" His response was, in essence, 'don't get caught up in that kind of process of intellectualisation, it leads you down all sorts of paths, and it usually leads you away from where you're trying to go'.

The Japanese connection with nature

These are the reasons why it's so valuable that we have contact with places like Japan, to give us that other side, and to show us that there is this bigger picture, that the Western way isn't necessarily the only way of doing it. I don't mean to invalidate a kind of Western approach, but I think it has its limitations.

In the West we're so focused on our visual sense that we tend to look at the exterior form and don't want to always interpret the interior form. But there's a deeper source, and in Japan, not just in gardens, they're constantly referring to 'going back to nature', as the source. So when you're looking at a garden, it's trying to understand our position as human beings to nature, and what that inter-relationship is, like Taoism. It's inclusive, very much so.

If you look at Japanese poetry, for example, the language is that of nature. They're all 'nature' images, and emotional states, and all the gradations of emotional states are expressed through images of nature. We don't tend to make those associations.

Culturally speaking, Japanese gardens are closer to nature than British gardens.

The Meiji period (1868-1912) and the switch from a feudal society to an industrialised modern society, which was relatively not very long ago, has had a huge impact on Japan. I think in Western civilisation we moved further along, further away from nature, earlier in time, whereas the Japanese still connect with nature, even if they live in the middle of Shinjuku! It's everywhere: you just go into a restaurant and eat the food, and the seasons are laid out for you on the plate! There's the little *okashi*, the sweets – in autumn they'll have autumn leaves on them, but go back in April and they'll have blossoms! We've tended to lose that, because we've had a fear of nature, nature was something that had to be dominated in Western culture. And that's how we've approached life, but in China and Japan it's been largely more a process of cooperation.

Sharing the experience

From 1994 to 1996 I taught at Tatton Park. I'd returned from Japan with not only a desire to create gardens, but was also so enthralled with what I'd learnt that I wanted to offer it to other people. I've never seen it as something which had been given to me, personally. It's something that comes through me, and so I've lectured, and taught classes, evening classes, and all sorts of things. The Tatton Park classes were reasonably well attended at the time but to be honest, it really wasn't much supported by the hierarchy, the management there, which is a shame. The 'School for Oriental Garden Studies' is a grand title, and they have a magnificent garden there, but I think we could have done more with it. But this was in the pre-internet days, so there was a limited exposure.

Doing the gardens here at Hatchmill Home, working with a group of volunteers, is another aspect of that urge to share; part of it to me is a kind of practical way of showing people how things can be done. That element of being a teacher is actually very important, I think, to transmit it. It's also that you begin to integrate that knowledge within yourself, because by teaching people, trying to explain what it is you're trying to do, or what you're trying to achieve, makes you think a little bit more clearly about what it is you are trying to do.

Healing gardens and show gardens

I have designed several gardens on the theme of healing, reflection and reconciliation. With the Japanese Garden Society, for example, we've built two gardens at Willowbrook Hospice near St Helens in Lancashire. I think 'reconciliation' is to do with 'dislocation'. Losing a family member can be a form of dislocation, and there's also this idea of dislocation from nature and from the natural environment, which is very damaging to society. For example, a lot of mental stress is caused when people live in the thirty-fifth floor of a tower block, or under the Heathrow flight path or even in the inner city; it's a desperate environment. A Japanese garden contains that healing element which I believe is very important in Western society.

I've had medals from the Royal Horticultural Society for show gardens, but I've never really pursued that. The RHS has a certain way of looking at gardens, which is different to mine. I once put some lilies in a Tatton Park show garden. They were unopened and that's how I wanted them, because they had the 'potential' of opening. And it was criticised and marked down. I would have received a Gold Medal had these lilies been fully opened, because that's how you're 'supposed' to display flowers! And that really incensed me, because it made me realise that we were thinking from totally different places. To me the beauty of that bud was the fact that it was opening rather than being open. That's where the beauty lay, the 'unseen' Zen aspect.

The Japanese Garden Society

Around 1992 I was part of a small group of people, most of whom were landscape architects, or students, or who had been architecture students in and around Manchester, and who had had some contact with Japan. We had a series of meetings at somebody's house, with the idea of "Wouldn't it be fun to create a Japanese Garden Society".

In 1993 we had the first 'official' meeting at Tatton Park and, much to everyone's utter amazement, about 200 people turned up from all over the UK! There had been a mention of it in the gardening section of the Saturday edition of the Telegraph, because Sam Yude who was the head gardener at Tatton Park, had contact with a journalist and they'd put a small paragraph to say there was going to be this meeting. I can't remember the wording, but it was something like '...to formulate a Japanese Garden Society', and the date. I think we anticipated something like fifteen people turning up, and the 200 people who came along were from all over the UK!

So that was the start of the Japanese Garden Society – and we celebrated our 20th anniversary in 2013. I've been involved ever since the beginning and was Chairman for a period. The aims of the Society are to promote a better understanding of the Japanese garden tradition, and there's also a very strong element of education in that, of creating the opportunity for people to experience Japanese gardens in their different forms, whether they be gardens that were created in the UK, like Tatton Park's historical garden, or in Japan. The Society is now a charity, and one of the main aims of the charitable status is that we have a strong educational element, to bring more and a deeper understanding of Japanese garden tradition.

It was also part of my remit to re-establish past historical Japanese gardens in the UK, to build up an accessible body of knowledge. There are still relatively few people who have had practical experience in Japan, which I think is pretty essential, but there's obviously a hunger. Media interest comes and goes, but beyond that it's very steady. I suspect that it's because we have this kind of 'dislocation' in the West between our relationship with nature and society. That points up a very good reason why people are interested in, and should be interested in, Japanese gardens, because it's a way of getting back into having a relationship, and a more profound relationship, with nature.

The first teahouse garden

In 1995 I created a *'Fugetsu-An'* teahouse for Raymond Blanc at his *Quat'Saisons* restaurant. If it has a theme it's in the name, 'Fugetsu-An', which means 'the love of nature'. It's a poetic term, made up of the characters for 'wind' (*fu*) and 'moon' (*getsu*); in fact, it's a haiku term which means 'the love of nature'.

At that time I wasn't so concerned with consciously using scenes, but since then I've become more interested in consciously introducing a scene, or a storyline, and exploiting the element of narrative that's possible in a garden. Raymond was very concerned that it ought to be as authentic as possible, which was kind of challenging, particularly with the planting, because it's quite an alkaline soil and the water is alkaline, so you can't grow azaleas. All the plants you would immediately reach for don't work there at all, so we had to use a lot of different ones. In 2013 I began re-planting this garden, and part of the process that I agreed for the refurbishment was that I wanted to train one of their staff, who would be specifically allocated to the garden.

Favourite gardens

Of all the different types of Japanese gardens I particularly love *kare sansui* [dry waterless] gardens. We created a garden at Norwich Cathedral which is a kind of hardcore *kare sansui* garden. There are no plants in it whatsoever; it is just a rock arrangement. It's very small, but I think it's one of the nicest gardens I've ever been involved with.

There's also a garden I did at a spa in California, which is more like a *kaiyushiki tei* garden which contains a narrative and tells a story, so as you walk around and experience the garden you go through the ten different stages of the Oxen, and the Ox Herder. It's a Buddhist parable that was particularly used in temples to teach people about the spiritual path; it's used a lot in Zen, and it is associated with Zen, but I think that its origins are much older than that. It appears in a form in Tibet as well, and also in India too, but with elephants rather than an ox. But it really came to life I guess in Zen temples in monasteries in China, and then also in Japan.

The creative process and a client's expectations

Creating a garden is very complex. I always thought that if I were a painter, life would be an awful lot simpler; I could just retire to my studio and create my piece of work, and not necessarily have a client!

I think you start with an undefined feeling of the space, and you listen to that and usually a picture emerges. You can see that in this garden here [at Hatchmill]. It's not a typical space where you would have a layout of a Japanese garden perhaps. There were limitations, there were restrictions that couldn't be changed and there were demands and expectations that Hatchmill brought to the process. So as a garden creator you have to balance all those, and then your own vision of what you see, and what you want to do.

It's a question of finding a balance between what the client expects and wants, and how you want it. You have your own vision of that space, so it is a compromise between the two. Very, very occasionally it happens that somebody will say, "Just build me something"; it's happened maybe twice in my life. On one occasion it was *carte blanche* with the cheque as well!

It's tempting to say that the ideal situation is where somebody just gives you *carte blanche*, creatively and financially to do what you want, but actually I think you get a better result where there are guidelines set down, or parameters set out and that creates the discipline. That's the framework, the structure which comes, and then you have to work within that, and it becomes more challenging. It does actually become a greater creative challenge, to come up with something then. But usually what happens is that by being in that space, some kind of picture starts to come into my mind, a kind of internal vision, and then the whole process of going through the design stage, and the building of the garden. I guess it extends even beyond that. It's all a question of refining that initial vision, which may not necessarily be very clear.

Usually you can sketch something out, but then when you start building it you don't necessarily refer to those sketches. Because you're working with actual materials themselves and I think it's a lot to do with taking the dominant mind – the garden creator – out of that process, and just letting it happen and go with the gut feeling. You are simply the vehicle through which it comes, that something becomes articulated. And the less you interfere with that process when you're in that flow, the better.

I have had several difficult clients! I have one client that I first met about twenty years ago, and back then he didn't want 'a Japanese garden', he wanted an English garden, and we started and I designed a garden which he was happy with. While we were building the garden I was getting four or five phone calls a day from him, and every time I turned up on site he would ask, "Why are you doing this? Why have you done that? What's happening here?" and this built up to a point that, to cut a long story short, we actually stood in the back garden chest to chest, screaming at each other until his wife came and dragged him into the house. I've never lost my temper, or my control, as I did with him; I felt I was on the point of hitting him and I've never hit anybody in my life! But the following day he apologised and recognised that he'd gone over the top and, since then, we've had a very good relationship. And I'm back there building another garden for him! There's no shouting now. He just says, "You do whatever you want, Robert, just don't make it too expensive, please!"

Success in garden design

People ask how I would define the success of a garden. I think if people recognise something of the spirit that you try to put in there, if something of the intangible becomes communicated, you know you're on the right path. It's not a question of getting awards, but of people making a connection with the garden. It may be that you don't necessarily recognise it yourself, because they see it in their own light, but it moves them in some way. It's more than emotion, it goes deeper, it comes out as an emotional response, but it actually comes from a deeper source. And when that happens, then you can think, 'Yeah, something's been done in the right way.' I always have that expectation, and I think – hope – it's getting better.

It's taken me a long time, and I'm still learning, and my apprenticeship is still going on! But I'm getting clearer about that myself, and I think it's a lot to do with how you prepare yourself to do the work. It took me a long time to really understand that. I heard it as an intellectual concept maybe thirty years ago, but I didn't really understand it as something you can actually incorporate into a piece of work and now I'm beginning to see that, and see that with my hands.

My favourite garden is usually the one I've just finished! And then a few weeks later you start looking at it, and think, 'Ah, that should have been there, or that could be changed!' I tend to be very critical, a bit hard in that way and I have on a couple of occasions been back to do something different. But I've seen gardens that I did fifteen, twenty years ago, which the client still likes, but I look at it and think, 'Oh God, that's awful!' 'I'd never do that now!' Of course you don't tell the client that! No, they are enjoying it for what it is.

Bridging cultures

Garden design can definitely promote the understanding of another culture; I think this is so important. Modernisation and globalisation are, in some senses, bringing cultures closer together, but it doesn't mean that an understanding and an appreciation of other cultures follow.

Gardens crystallise so much of culture; so many different aspects of culture come together. You could equally point to the tea ceremony, *Cha no yu*, as being a distillation of Japanese culture every bit as much as the gardens. But I think particularly for English people, gardens bridge the gap, because we have such a close association with gardens. And there's this fantastic body of knowledge, we can expand our consciousness by looking at other cultures, and learning from other cultures. It's been my experience that this process has happened, without necessarily even trying.

I never wanted to replicate what I've seen in Kyoto, but, buried in there, or contained within that tradition there is a whole raft of ideas, and concepts, and ways of thinking that are transcultural. They are beyond culture. And that's what we can take, and to try and implant into a different culture. So it actually doesn't belong to the culture. When I build a garden in England it belongs to the culture of England, but it utilises those ideas that are coming through the Japanese garden tradition, rather than trying to copy something that you would see in Japan, and just make a replica. It involves those elements, but it's the way that it's done. Now I begin to understand that it's actually an interior process, it's not just simply to do with the external form, it's actually an internal process – and that's also why it takes a long time to create a gardener, or to create any kind of craftsman, or artist.

For the future

I would like to be better at what I do. I'm really enjoying building the kind of gardens like the one at Hatchmill which are in public, or semi-public, spaces. You know some people come here and they don't leave, they die here. People come here with terminal illness, and I want to explore and develop that aspect of it more. I'm trying to find more places where I can help to create a kind of healing garden, to create an oasis of calmness, or stillness, however you call it, that might just touch on somebody's life.

The last day when we were building the garden here, one of the resident patients, a lady in a wheelchair, was out in the garden, watching us. Everyone was rushing around clearing up, and she was right in the middle of the path, so we had to wheel the wheelbarrows around her, and she kept on saying, "I'm in the way, aren't I?" I said to her several times, "No, no, you stay where you are, you're fine." It was funny, because my initial thought was irritation – "Oh, she's in the way!" – and then coming out of that, and realising there was another whole aspect of it, and maybe it was quite important that she was there. For about an hour or so, she just sat in her wheelchair, and we were all weaving around her.

Afterwards I realised that there had been this sense of her static-ness; her sitting there, was like a rock, she became part of the garden, and something of the quality of her stillness was actually becoming part of the fabric of the garden. That was the spot of stillness, like the *Fudo Myoo*, the 'Immoveable One', and she just got caught in it and couldn't really move, and to have been off the path would have disturbed her. It was a beautiful moment, it was really lovely. If people can get something of that, even just the merest little whiff of that, then I think that is the beginning of the healing process, or a process of reconciliation.

I'm still trying to combine East and West; it's an unfolding process. I've been doing this for about thirty years now, and I'm still trying! I've gone through the process of being very absorbed by technique, of wanting to learn about the history of Japanese gardens, the history of Japan, and all different aspects of Japanese culture. And now where I'm at is actually letting go of a lot of that, in a sense. To just let it come out somehow, and I think I've got sufficient experience now to be able to start to do that.

Part of me has this enormous sense of gratitude to Japan, and to Kyoto, because it gave me a quality of life, or distilled, or brought into being a creative life, and I feel very honoured to be able to put that out into the world, however badly or well I might do it. It's part of that connection with Japan. I feel a huge sense of gratitude for what I was given, the opportunity I was given. It's a love affair!

ROBERT KETCHELL

Garden Designer and Author, Co-founder of the Japan Garden Society

	Born Cheshire, England; family visit to Tatton Park at an early age
1970s	Studied at Askham Bryan College in Yorkshire; lived and worked in London
1980s	Visited Japan en route to India, stopped and stayed in Kyoto, became apprentice to a master gardener and studied at Kyoto University for three years
1986	Returned to Cheshire and started a landscaping business, Robert Ketchell Garden Design
1993	Co-founded the Japan Garden Society, became chairman over several years; the JGS celebrated 20 years in 2013 with special edition of *Shakkei* magazine
1994-96	Teaching post at Tatton Park in the School of Oriental Garden Design
1995	Designed tea garden *Fugetsu-an* for Raymond Blanc at *Le Manoir aux Quatr' Saisons* restaurant – later redevelopment of tea garden in 2013/14
2000s	Designed and built many garden projects in the UK, Europe and the USA in California; won medals at the Royal Horticultural Society shows for garden design
2001	Published book *Japanese Gardens in a Weekend* (Hamlyn Press)
2007	Created the Garden of 'Reflection & Reconciliation for Willowbrook Hospice
2008	Acted as consultant for many TV programmes on Japanese gardens including *Around the World in 80 Gardens* by Monty Don for the BBC in 2008
2010	Created Garden of Contemplation at Norwich Cathedral, with new Hostery buildings opened by HM The Queen

2013   Created Japanese garden at Hatchmill Care Home, Farnham, England

2015   Continues to work in garden design for private and commercial projects in Britain, Europe, the USA and Japan, with a particular focus on healing gardens

AWARDS

Won several medals for the JGS at the Royal Horticultural Society's garden shows

Hatch Mill Hospice Japanese garden, Farnham 2013

JUNKO KOBAYASHI

CONCERT PIANIST, CO-FOUNDER AND FORMER CHAIR OF THE TAKEMITSU SOCIETY IN THE UK

"When I was studying, people always asked me to play something from Japan, but I always thought the Takemitsu pieces were the ones that I wanted to play. So I started with one piece, and then more and more, and I always liked his music very much.

"I think Takemitsu had a really original way of writing music, and he said his mentor was Debussy, so his sound is very French, so when they didn't know that was Takemitsu, people would say 'Oh, is that Debussy?'"

Junko Kobayashi

The early years

When I was five years old, we were living in Kyoto. One of the ladies who worked in the same bank as my father was learning to play the piano, and one day I went with my mother to watch her play in a pupils' concert. I don't remember what they were playing, but it was a concert in the YWCA hall in Kyoto, a big place, and person after person, mainly children, played on a grand piano. I remember very well that on the way back we were crossing what seemed a huge road, and my mother asked me, "Well, would you like to learn to play the piano too?" and I said, "Yes". So, inspired by that concert, I began my musical life.

I started with a piano teacher in Kyoto and after a year or so we moved to Kobe because my father was transferred to the Kobe branch of the bank. There I took lessons from Machiko Asahina, the wife of Professor Takashi Asahina, a great conductor who had an international reputation. He has passed away now, but he was very well known at the time.

My parents didn't have any ambition for me to become a professional pianist. For my part, I was just going to piano lessons, enjoying them, and practised every day. The only concerts I played in were the pupils' concerts every year. I was not ambitious, not at all.

My mother's side of the family was always very musical. My great-grandfather was of the first generation that played the violin, a European instrument; and my grandmother also played violin. My mother's sisters all played piano and sang in choirs and so on. My father's side of the family was not at all musical when I was a child, although my father became a keen chorister later on.

Studying in Germany, coming to London

After I started learning piano with Machiko Asahina I went on to study at the Osaka College of Music, where she was a professor, but I was still not sure whether I wanted to become a professional pianist. After my graduation, Professor and Mrs Asahina said that they thought I should go to Germany to study. So I went to the *Folkwang Universität der Künste*, in Essen. Even when I graduated from there, I was full of doubt about my ability. But my professors suggested that I study further in London with a particular teacher, Maria Curcio. It was only when I came to London in 1980 that I became more focused and serious about becoming a pianist. So I was really a very slow developer!

Before London, however, I spent a term at university in Düsseldorf, studying philosophy. I was buying time, and wanted to find out what I really wanted to do. But I regret to say that I didn't understand much of what I studied, or tried to study, in Düsseldorf!

However, I was due to give a little concert in a small town in Germany, and thought that I shouldn't cancel it. So I started to practice again, and played the concert, and that made me think, "Whether I like it or not, whether I'm good at it or not, this is what I am here for." So that was a sort of turning point, just before I came to London.

Musical influences

I think it just happened that I have stayed in England; I didn't plan to stay so long in this country! I came to study first, with Maria Curcio, and then I went on to study with Louis Kentner. Maria was a renowned teacher. She herself had been taught by Artur Schnabel and by Nadia Boulanger; she had played with Benjamin Britten, Otto Klemperer and Elizabeth Schwartzkopf; and her pupils included Martha Argerich, Radu Lupu, and Mitsuko Uchida. Louis Kentner was born in Hungary. He had been asked by Bartok to play the first performances of his second and third piano concertos, and had been asked by the BBC to broadcast all of the Beethoven piano sonatas. He often played and recorded with his brother-in-law Yehudi Menuhin. I was enormously lucky to be taught by such exceptional musicians.

My first big public performance in England was in 1988. I made my debut with the London Philharmonic Orchestra at the Royal Festival Hall. I had played some small recitals before, for example in Burgh House in Hampstead, or in the church in Rosslyn Hill. Was I nervous for my first big public performance? Yes, very, as you can imagine, playing with such a highly regarded orchestra in such a big hall! And then I began to play concerts all over the world – in Tokyo and New York, and also in

Caracas, Cracow, Lusaka, Schumen, and so on. I even appeared on American television.

And I also started to teach. Life revolved around concerts and teaching. I taught a lot of children and adults. Yes, I enjoyed teaching very much.

Breaking down musical cultural barriers

When I was growing up in Japan we heard some recordings of Japanese traditional music in music lessons at school, but it was predominantly a *Western* musical education. When my mother was young, before marrying, she used to play the *Koto*; when I was a child she still had the instrument but I never heard her playing it. On the other hand, my first memory of listening to music was my mother's record of Arthur Rubinstein playing Beethoven's *Emperor* concerto, and a record of arias from *La Traviata*. So I had absolutely no idea about Japanese music as my upbringing was with Western music.

When I was studying in Germany, a big problem for me was interpreting Western music, because German people think that music, especially by Bach, Beethoven and Brahms, is *their* music.

I remember an occasion when one of my fellow music students asked me, "Why are you actually here? What are you doing here? Why do you play Western music?" That sort of attitude!

It was an issue for me that I was Japanese interpreting Western music. But when I came to London I felt better about it, because the first thing that struck me was that going to a concert in the Festival Hall or Wigmore Hall or wherever, there were so many artists from all over the world playing Western classical music in their own style. For example, a Latin-American pianist will play Beethoven in a very different way from a German pianist playing Beethoven.

So I have reconciled myself to this: you can do it your way, you don't have to be born into it. And the world has changed so much since I first came to England in 1980; so many different nationalities of artists come to perform. Now there are so many Chinese pianists, you know, so nobody thinks like that anymore.

Those restrictions have been broken down and it's become much more global.

Nigel Kennedy

One good thing about London is that by chance my neighbour was Nigel Kennedy. Despite his appearance and behaviour, Nigel is a true and wonderful musician. I played with him and have learned a lot from him. When I knew him best he was at the height of his fame. It was in 1989 that he made his *Four Seasons* recording with the ECO. He had an incredible 'star' lifestyle, but he also worked very, very hard, and sometimes practised all night. So I really admire him very much.

The Takemitsu Society

When I was studying, even when I was studying in Germany, people always asked me to play something from Japan. So I went through all the piano music by Japanese composers, but I always thought the Takemitsu pieces were the ones that I wanted to play. I started with one of his pieces, and then with more and more, and I always liked his music very much.

Then in 1996 I played a little Japanese concert in the Arts Club in London. On this occasion, I played some Takemitsu pieces, together with pieces by Debussy which had some Oriental influence. The Japanese *Shakuhachi* (flute) player, Yoshikazu Iwamoto, who lectured at York University, came and played in this concert too. After the concert I had tea with the promoter, and I was talking enthusiastically to him about Takemitsu. Then he asked, 'Why don't *we* start a Takemitsu Society? Is he still alive?" Actually, Takemitsu had just died, so the promoter thought that we should start a society and maybe do a memorial concert. So, a year later, we gave a *Homage to Takemitsu* concert in St John's Smith Square.

Meanwhile, the promoter kindly organised meetings with other societies – with people from the Beethoven Society, the Liszt Society and so on. They told us how to start and how to run a society. We had done all this preparation, but then the promoter unfortunately became ill. It was a pity to throw all the preparation away, and then, at about this time, I met Peter Burt who was just finishing his PhD thesis on Toru Takemitsu. He knew everything about Takemitsu, is a gifted lecturer, and together we started the Society. The Daiwa Anglo-Japanese Foundation was very helpful, and gave us their salon to do the first event. They hosted our inaugural concert and a film show in their premises in 1997, and so with their help we got started.

Takemitsu's work fascinates me because he has his own sort of musical language. There were so many other Japanese composers copying Western music and then writing in Japanese style. I think Takemitsu actually created a really original way of writing music, and he said his mentor was Debussy, so obviously his sound is very French. So when you don't know that was Takemitsu, people say, "Oh, is that Debussy?" At the same time it's not just an imitation, and, as Peter Burt says, in every piece there's this Japanese concept of *Ma* (space), and it's always there in the piano pieces as well, and that is really wonderful. Even when he uses dissonant chords or very sharp sounds he had such a fine ear that the sound he creates is really beautiful.

Takemitsu was always very conscious about differences between Western culture and Oriental or Japanese culture; he was always thinking about it. For him, to create his own new music was like 'hatching a global egg'. As early as the 1960s he wrote a piece for orchestra with two Japanese soloists, that was commissioned by the New York Philharmonic when Ozawa Seiji was the conductor there. Takemitsu used a *biwa* (the Japanese lute) and a *shakuhachi* (flute) as solo instruments. It was called *November Steps*. Now that we have all sorts of world music, it would be quite normal; 'Fusion' music and all that has become very, very, common. But at that time when he wrote this piece in 1967, it was *so* sensational, and so experimental, it was really amazing. I think he was really revolutionary in the 1960s, and that fascinates me about him. I was chair of the Takemitsu Society from 1997 to 2013, when it was passed on to Peter Burt.

Favourite composers

I have several favourite composers. I play a lot of Beethoven, and I feel quite a natural affinity to his music. I think it suits me, but also I love playing Chopin, and I like playing Liszt. I have a lot of memories of Liszt pieces because my second teacher in London, Louis Kentner, was one of the greatest Liszt players, so I learned a lot from him.

I don't have any favourite orchestras; each one I work with is different. And each conductor is so different that each orchestra has its own character and personality, so usually I fit in with that.

I also like jazz very much. I don't play it, but when I'm in the kitchen I always put some jazz on. I love it. I'm not that knowledgeable, but I like Count Basie, Dave Brubeck and Art Tatum; and I also like the American singer Blossom Dearie who lived in France. I saw Ella Fitzgerald at the Barbican, but that was much later. We are quite a musical block here – there's another pianist, and a porter and a gardener who sing in the local choir!

Ongoing Projects

A big project in my life is recording three of Beethoven's piano sonatas, led by the *Appassionata*, and including *Op.2 No 1* and *Op.110*. I plan to record a further three of his sonatas, including the *Waldstein*, in 2015. Beethoven is a core effort, it's a real challenge. Getting the personality of the composer, I think it is quite challenging.

I'm also keen on doing chamber music, and have performed for the first time in public concert music for four hands with a brilliant young Lithuanian pianist. We played some Schubert, *Fantasie*, and Mozart *Sonata*. It's a new genre for me and it's great fun. I'm also playing with a singer and doing all sorts of songs by Schubert and Mozart, and other things, so there's a lot of music to learn.

Since 2007 I have played one or two concerts a year in the admirable David Josefowitz Hall at the Royal College of Music and I would like to continue this series, as well as performing out of London. I'm playing more mainstream repertoire now, as well as Takemitsu of course, and I just really want to get better at playing music.

A Japanese life in London

Would I go back to Japan to live? Oh well, I must ask my husband Gerald! At the moment I cannot actually think about going back. But when I do go back, I really enjoy being there. I go once or twice a year; usually to play a concert and see my family. And I always wish I could stay a bit longer.

I think London is the real centre of music worldwide. The variety of the concerts and the quality of the music in London is incredible. So it's good to be here, because you're always stimulated by the great artists who perform here.

London is exceptionally cosmopolitan, so that for *me* it is very comfortable living here. Every afternoon troops of little Japanese children are shepherded from a local school. In our local library they have a section of Japanese books. Opposite, a grocery shop sells Japanese food. On the stand, Japanese newspapers. In the High Street, a Japanese restaurant. Across the road, a Japanese clinic. I go to a French class and an exercise class *jiriku seitai* in the Nippon Club. I have made Japanese friends through these classes, and they enrich my life. I feel I'm very fortunate because I have an English life and a parallel Japanese life, which is absolutely wonderful!

JUNKO KOBAYASHI

Concert Pianist, Co-founder and Former Chair of the Takemitsu Society in the UK

	Started learning piano at the age of five in Kyoto
1968	Studied at the Osaka College of Music
1970s	Graduated in music at the *Folkwang Universität der Künste*, University of Ruhr Essen, Germany
	Studied Philosophy at the University of Düsseldorf
1980	Came to London to study piano with Maria Curcio, then studied with Louis Kentner
1988	Debut with the London Philharmonic Orchestra at the Royal Festival Hall London
	Thereafter gives recitals in London at the Royal Academy of Music, the Wigmore Hall, the Purcell Room, St John's Smith Square and other venues
1996	Played chamber music recital with Nigel Kennedy
1997	Founded the Takemitsu Society with musicologist Peter Burt ; chairman of the Takemitsu Society for 15 years
2000s	Made concert tours of Great Britain, France, Germany, Denmark, Bulgaria, Poland, USA, Canada, Venezuela, Zambia, Thailand and Japan
2007	Started giving regular recitals in the David Josefowitz Hall at the Royal College of Music
2012	Started recording the Beethoven *Sonatas*; extended her repertoire to include playing in chamber music ensembles and accompanying singers
2015	Recorded three further Beethoven sonatas, including the *Waldstein*; continues to give many concerts internationally and in London and record new works

ORCHESTRAS WORKED WITH

> London Philharmonic Orchestra
>
> Osaka Philharmonic Orchestra
>
> Caracas Municipal Symphony Orchestra
>
> Polish Baltic Symphony Orchestra
>
> And many others

TV & BROADCASTS

> ZDF TV in Germany
>
> WKAR TV in the USA
>
> BBC R3 in the UK

CDs

> 1993 *Junko Kobayashi plays Chopin & Liszt* (Pegasus – PGS101-2)
>
> 2004 *Nocturnes* (Quartz – QTZ 2004)
>
> 2013 *Beethoven: The Appassionata Sonata* plus piano sonatas 1 and 31 (k576 Music Ltd – k576121)
>
> 2015 *Beethoven: The Waldstein Sonata* plus piano sonatas op.31-3 and op. 109 (k576 Music Ltd – k576148)

Junko Kobayashi practising at home, 2011

SETSUO KATO

PHOTO JOURNALIST AND PUBLISHER, ARCHIVIST OF THE JAPANESE COMMUNITY IN THE UK

"Japan is a democratic country, and we share a lot of common things with Britain, like the royal family, and no resources; we have to manufacture things, the people are important, and education is important. The Japanese are doing very well, and Britain is a model for the Japanese."

"And also the difference is Japanese women. They are much more independent now. To me the Japanese women are doing very well, and are very international, wherever you go. I think after Panasonic and Toyota, the best Japanese export is women actually! They're a very good Japanese export!"

Setsuo Kato

News photographer

I was studying journalism at Waseda University in Tokyo when I heard that a British news agency was looking for a university graduate. I was interested in taking the job. However, I did not know that Keystone Press was a news photo agency and I became a news photographer from day one. Though I expected to be reporting news in words, I had to forget about writing for a while. For three and a half years I photographed accidents, incidents, demonstrations, politicians, fashion shows and various big events including members of the British royal family visiting Japan.

I particularly remember the Beatles coming to Japan in 1967. I went to the *Budokan* to take photographs of them and to the press conference held at the Hilton Hotel where they stayed. Keystone Press wanted a scoop photo of the Beatles in Japan. We asked the owner of the Air France building which stood opposite the Hilton Hotel and arranged for our photographers to take photographs from across the street of the Beatles who might come out onto the balcony of their Penthouse room at the Hilton. Keystone photographers including myself took turns on the top floor of the Air France building. I managed to take several photographs of the Beatles who came out on the balcony to look around. They were good pictures and were sent worldwide through Keystone's network. These photographs were not credited to me or the other photographers, but to Keystone Press.

This made me think that being a freelance photographer would be more interesting, as you can put your name on your work, rather than a company's name, so I quit and became freelance. But you don't get jobs just because you suddenly declare you have become freelance, so I had to do something about it. Because Keystone was a British news agency, I was interested in England. Also I liked the Beatles and I wanted to learn the English language, so I decided to go to London for a year.

Coming to London in 1970

I left Japan in 1970 and the journey to England took a long time. The cheapest way to go to Europe was via Siberia. I took a Russian boat from Yokohama to Nokhodka and then travelled by

Siberian railway. I visited several European countries before coming to London and it took me more than three weeks. When I arrived in London my hair, beard and moustache were all very long and I looked very messy! I thought I wouldn't be allowed into the reputed "gentleman's country". But amazingly, the immigration officer had long hair, the policemen had beards and moustaches, and people in general were rather untidy-looking. So I just mingled in very well! I thought "What a fantastic country!" It was in the middle of the flower power era and Carnaby Street was flourishing. I became a kind of early Japanese 'flower child', who wore striped *'rappa-zubon'*, (bell-bottom jeans) and a butterfly necklace, which was very trendy at that time.

That was how I came here and settled. I came totally on my own. I didn't ask any help from Keystone Press in Tokyo nor in London. I just came here basically for one year to look around and to learn English. But after about ten months, towards the end of the first year, I met an English lady, Jill Fanshawe, and that is in a sense the reason I am still here. I had a column in a Japanese magazine called 'Current English Journal' published by *Kenkyusha*. Every month I had to send one topic from London. The column was called 'London Calling'. The feature for one month was 'English people learning Japanese in London'. I went to a language school in Holborn which had a Japanese course and I interviewed Jill. That was how I met her. She already spoke Japanese very well, which was very impressive. Now that was over forty years ago. I wanted to stay here more than a year, but you could not just study English all the time, so I joined a private college, the College of Journalism in Fleet Street. I studied photo-journalism there and professional photographers and journalists came to teach, which was quite useful, and I learned how to be a photo-journalist.

A different way of working

In the beginning it was difficult working in London because of the language problem, and also the system was quite different. In Japan, if you went out to do a job, for example interviewing company directors or politicians, every question should be handed in beforehand. They didn't do things spontaneously. But here it was more spontaneous, in a sense more free and easy-going. Of course you had to make an appointment to see people and roughly explain what you were going to ask, but often end up by asking wider questions. Sometimes it was difficult to make an appointment, but once you got it, it worked very well.

There were other obstacles. When I did a job interviewing British companies, they often did not hesitate to say, "Oh Japanese coming – be careful! They copy everything!" That was what their reaction was at the time. They don't do it any more. Also I often heard somebody saying, "Remember Pearl Harbour!" It was only twenty-five years after the end of WW2, and it was still in people's minds. The Japanese themselves were still very ashamed of the war and the British were very proud of victory. Britain in the 1970s was still having that sort of feeling toward the Japanese. When you bought a cheap box of matches at a supermarket, you often found the matches were 'Made in Japan'. Japanese goods had a reputation of being "cheap and nasty". Now you get quite the opposite reaction to Japanese goods. The Japanese have been working very hard to achieve a good reputation for the last forty years.

Photography

Photography has been an important part of my life. I was totally surprised when I first came across a Western photographer in Japan. While I was working as a photographer at Keystone Press in Tokyo, the American nuclear aircraft carrier 'Enterprise' visited Yokosuka, and I was sent to take photographs. There was a big anti-nuclear demonstration and demonstrators and riot police were clashing. I was instinctively lured into the battlefield and took photographs. It was raining heavily and I was absolutely soaked, but I managed to take some good shots.

Later, on the way back to the railway station, I noticed an American photographer taking photographs of one of the demonstrators squeezing the water out of a big banner which was totally wet. It was not on the battlefield, but in a calm situation. I realised the photographer had captured the essence of the demonstration. The battle was, of course, a very important aspect for a news photograph, but the aftermath of the storm was too. Particularly if you are doing a feature, you need quite a few different aspects. I learned a lot from that scene. News photographers tend to photograph more sensational scenes, but there is always a different aspect. Photographers should capture that aspect as well as sensational scenes. I learnt that this sort of photography was fairer and also more creative.

One Sunday I went to the beach in Kamakura with the senior photographer at Keystone Press. It was a beautiful day and everyone was sitting on the beach. But suddenly a big wave came and a small child was swept away into the sea. Everyone stood up and tried to help, but my senior photographer was calm and started taking photographs of the child. I had a camera but I rushed to the sea and did not even think of taking photographs. I was so embarrassed for not helping the child, and also not taking photographs. I was still young and inexperienced, but I thought I had learnt what a professional photographer was about.

I was trained as a journalist and became a news photographer in Tokyo. When I came to London, I found photographs published in the British newspapers were quite different from Japanese ones. There were more creative photographs being published in English newspapers. In Japan newspapers use more informative photographs, and a photograph should include all the information. But here in Britain there is more emphasis on the individual photographer's eye. Photographs here are an equal to the articles, while in Japan photographs seem to be used to support articles. British photographers express their own eye on the news and the results are more creative.

Return to Tokyo

I went back to Tokyo for a while in 1974 because I was losing my contacts with the Japanese press which meant losing my market. Also I wanted to establish myself in Japan as a freelance photo-journalist. I had good Japanese photographer friends in Japan and we set up a freelance photographers' agency called Eva Press. We had a small office in Roppongi in the middle of Tokyo. We rented the top floor of a very old three-storied apartment. The area was residential and did not have many shops or restaurants. Eva Press does not exist anymore, and our office building was demolished to build the 54-storey Mori building in Roppongi Hills.

So I went back to establish the press agency and Jill came with me to Tokyo. I wanted to marry her in Japan and asked her to come, but she was not very happy to come to Japan. She had lived there before I met her in London, and she didn't much like Japanese society. In fact she didn't like Japanese men particularly! Anyway, I asked her to come and she gave me two conditions; if I cleared those conditions, then she might come. The first condition was that I should find her a good pottery teacher with whom she could study. And the other one was to give her a return ticket so she could come back any time. I passed these two conditions and she came, and we were married in Japan. It was a traditional Shinto style wedding with me in *hakama* and her in *kimono*. She studied pottery intensively there and that was her base, then and now, as a professional ceramic artist. She had studied painting at Chelsea and she was teaching art in a London school when I met her for the first time.

Developing as an international photo-journalist

We came back to London to settle in 1977. I wanted to establish myself as an international photo-journalist based in Europe. Many Japanese young people then wanted to go to the States, but I didn't like America. I hated American culture, namely; Coca cola, chewing gum and American teenagers! So it was Europe and in particular, I wanted to live in London. I started working as a photo-journalist for Japanese news media including newspapers, magazines, books and radio and television. Japan was enjoying its bubble economy in the 1980s and those years were flourishing years for freelance photo-journalists working for the Japanese media, which covered wider international news and affairs, and freelancers like me were sent to every corner of Europe and often to the States. The 1980s were an incredibly busy decade for me. I was sent to Paris for a day to take one photograph to put on the front cover of some magazine and to Madrid the next day to interview a Japanese artist living there. I had an assignment to introduce 12 small countries in Europe which included Monaco, the Vatican and Iceland. I took photographs of Margaret Thatcher's election campaign and the wedding of Prince Charles and Lady Diana. The Japanese Crown Prince studied at Oxford for two years and I photographed him from the entrance ceremony to the time he left from Heathrow Airport.

My articles and photographs have been published in most established news papers and magazines in Japan. Thirteen of my books on various subjects have also been published. It was a good time with lots of jobs, but toward the end of the '80s I was getting very tired. Going abroad including the States 15-16 times a year and also driving to various parts of Britain to take photographs and interview people was very tiring. Also I had to go back to Japan two or three times a year to keep in touch with the Japanese media. I felt exhausted and knew I couldn't carry on that way.

The Nichi-Ei Times

Towards the end of the '80s I decided to reduce my workload a bit. In 1990 I started selecting only good jobs and refused other minor jobs. When I studied journalism at Waseda, my dream was to have and publish my own newspaper. With the support of my friend Toshiko Marks I started my own newspaper in London called *"The Nichi-Ei Times"* in 1991, aiming at Japanese residents in the UK.

Every local region in Japan has its own newspaper, such as the *Kyoto Shimbun* or the *Hokkaido Shimbun*. I saw there was no local Japanese newspaper as such here, yet so many things were happening in the Japanese community which consisted of about 50,000 residents in the UK at that time. Many Japanese business establishments were operating here and a lot of famous people from Japan were visiting London. There was no shortage of news to write about. Also I thought it was easier for me to stay in London rather than going to France or Spain all the time. I wanted to publish my own newspaper to inform Japanese people about what was happening in the Japanese community in the UK, to record those events for the future, to introduce people who formed the Japanese community and to help Japanese people to understand British systems and life-style. Two other papers existed at that time, 'News Digest', and *'London Dayori'*, but they had no journalists working for them. They used translations of English news into Japanese and did not present community news.

What I wanted to create was a local newspaper for community news like they had in Japan.

I tried to sell the paper for £1 a copy, but hardly any people bought it. Why? Because if you asked the shops to stock my newspaper, they put it next to the News Digest and the *London Dayori* which were both free with nice glossy paper in full colour. On the contrary, my paper was just like an ordinary newspaper printed in black and white on rather poor quality paper, so nobody bought it!

I remember someone from Japan Airlines suggesting that I had two or three wrong concepts with the paper. He said, "Why don't you print more, even if you are wasting paper?", "Employ a good salesman and take more advertisements" and finally, "*Kato-san*, you are a good journalist but it does not mean you are a good businessman!" So I printed 5,000 copies and made it free. People started picking it up and more advertisements came in. Soon I increased to 10,000 copies and it was successful.

But towards the end of the 1990s the Japanese economy really shrank and big companies like Asahi Shimbun, JSTV, Japan Airlines and ANA were all cutting their advertising budgets, and it became more and more difficult to run the paper. I employed about twenty freelance journalists with five in the office for the production and it cost a lot. It was quite a big operation. It came to the stage I could not carry on publishing anymore, so I decided to cease the publication in 2002.

The Japanese Embassy felt very sorry to see the Nichi-Ei Times disappearing. Minister Oku – later Ambassador Oku when he was killed in Iraq – was a fellow Waseda man and we got on very well. He particularly felt sorry for me and suggested that the Embassy could purchase some of the photographs I had taken for the Embassy records. A few thousand pounds came in to support the Nichi-Ei Times debt. Minister Takeuchi, the Director of JICC at the Embassy told me, "It's a pity to stop it, but you've done it for ten years. Why don't we keep all the publications of the paper in the Japanese Embassy Library?" All issues spanning 10 years were kept there, and the Minister also wrote to the National Diet Library in Japan to keep the copies of the newspaper. The British Library also wanted to keep them as a record of the Japanese community in the late 20th century in the UK. At the end all publications of the Nichi-Ei Times were kept in British and Japanese national libraries, the Japanese Embassy Library in London and the Japan Society Library. It was lucky I had kept several copies of every issue from the beginning for the purpose of recording the history of the Japanese community in Britain.

I thought it would be easy to publish a newspaper, but it transpired that it was not. It was easy to fill pages with articles and photographs, but it was difficult to run as a business. I started the newspaper to ease my freelance jobs, but ended up busier and more tired than before. I learned a lesson that I may be an able photo-journalist but not an able businessman.

Producing books

From the 1970s onwards thirteen of my books have been published in Japan. A couple of books were about Scotch malt whisky. A Japanese publisher, *Shincho-sha*, asked me if I'd be interested in doing a feature on Scotch malt whisky. When I said "Yes", they told me I had to visit one hundred and twenty distilleries in Scotland. That meant I had to visit *every* distillery in Scotland! It took me six weeks, and they were not in Edinburgh or Glasgow, they were in the Orkneys, in Skye, on other islands and remote Highland areas. I had to drive to get there. Once I got there, I had to take photographs, interview the managers, and then go to the next one. Sometimes I had to visit four distilleries a day. It was a fantastic job, really! I published numerous articles and photographs on Scotch whisky in various Japanese magazines as well as two specialist books. Since then I have done quite a few whisky lectures in London. My other books include several London guides, photo-books on British children and the Lake District, photo-essays and a couple of "How to speak English" books. Two life-style books called *London Life-Style Vols.1 & 2* were written in English and illustrated by my wife Jill. I published a *London Walking Guide*fvery in 2013. I would like to spend more time writing books in future.

Development of the UK-Japanese relationship

When I came here in 1970 anywhere I went, people automatically regarded me as a Chinese. The British people had no idea about Japanese people living in this country. One day when I was in Leicester, a grandmother and a little girl asked me if I was from Hong Kong. I told them I was Japanese and the grandmother was so surprised and told her granddaughter, "You see! Today we have seen a Japanese man!" It sounded as if they had seen a strange animal in the zoo and I did not feel comfortable at all. But this kind of thing doesn't happen here anymore.

Because I've been here for a long time, people often ask me if Britain or London has changed in the last 40 years. To me, it is Japan that has changed more than here. Japan, particularly Tokyo where I come from, is incredibly different from forty years ago when I left. In London people's life styles may have changed, but the buildings and town layouts haven't changed much. Tokyo has totally transformed into a new city and you could not recognise it if you had been away for some time. People's minds have changed as well. My wife Jill noticed this too. When she lived in Tokyo a long time ago, she was called *"Gaijin!"* or *"Amerikajin!"* wherever she went and kids pointed at her, but now in Tokyo nobody takes any notice of her. If you spoke a word in Japanese forty years ago, everyone was shocked and would say "Oh fantastic! You speak Japanese!" But now if you say *"Konnichiwa, Ogenkidesuka"* in Japanese, most Japanese people just reply *"Arigato Gozaimasu"* . That is good, because the Japanese have become more international.

Another difference is Japanese women. They are much more independent now. Every year in the UK, there are around three hundred registrations of Japanese nationals marrying non-Japanese nationals at the Japanese Embassy in London. Most of the Japanese nationals are women, and there are several hundred children born here with a Japanese mother and British father. They can have dual nationality until they are twenty-one; then they have to choose. To me Japanese women are doing very well and have become very international. Wherever I go from the north of Scotland to the south-west of England, I find Japanese women living there with their British husbands. I think after Panasonic and Toyota, the best Japanese export is women, actually! They are very popular and high quality, like Japanese cars!

Both Japan and Britain are democratic countries and we share a lot of common things, such as being island countries, having a long history, a royal family, and similar political and economic systems. Both countries have limited natural resources and people's skills are very important. Britain has been a model for the Japanese for a long time and now we think we are equal and must cooperate and help each other in many fields.

In the 1980s Nissan set up a factory in Sunderland in the north-east of England. British people's opinions were divided. Some people, particularly in the south, thought it was an invasion of the Japanese car industry, but others including the Prime Minister, Margaret Thatcher welcomed Nissan because it created new jobs and also it introduced a new way of management to manufacturing industries. I think that Nissan's success changed the British people's attitude toward Japanese companies and Japanese people in general.

The Japanese Festival

In 1985 I was involved in organising the Japanese Summer Festival (*Natsu-Matsuri*) in London. There was a social organisation called *Anjin-kai* (named after Miura Anjin = William Adams who was the first Briton to arrive in Japan in 1600). Members were mostly young British people who had been to Japan and taught English on the BET (British Exchange Teachers) Programme which was a predecessor of the present JET Programme. The chair of Anjin-kai, Sue Hudson, had been in Mishima, Shizuoka-ken for a few years. She greatly enjoyed *Natsu-Matsuri* there and was keen to create a Japanese style summer festival in London. She asked me to co-organise a festival.

It was a hard work. Japan was not in British people's minds. Although the tea ceremony and flower arrangement were known, popular Japanese performing cultures such as *Bon-Odori*, *Taiko* and *Roten* (stalls) were simply not known in this country. After much struggle and devotion the first Anglo-Japanese Summer Festival was launched at Battersea Park in August 1985. We built a *Yagura* stage in the middle of the park and had *Taiko, Bon-Odori, Hanabi*

(Japanese fireworks) and other stage acts. We had a lot of stalls selling Japanese food. To our surprise, the Japanese Crown Prince who was studying at Oxford at the time, came and joined the Bon-Odori dance with the people, which was a fantastic endorsement for the festival.

I photographed the Crown Prince on many occasions while he was at Oxford University. I often talked to him when I photographed. I wanted to talk to him more, but his *Jiju*, chamberlain, always stopped me by saying "Kato-san, it's enough!" He was a very nice and sincere person and interested in conversation. Personally I liked him very much, but it is a pity that back in Japan now, he does not have the kind of freedom he enjoyed while in the UK.

The annual *Natsu-Matsuri* lasted for 10 years and was very successful in promoting Anglo-Japanese cultural relationships. This was really the first time to introduce Japanese grassroots culture to the UK. Today we have an established Japan Matsuri annually in London and many other Japanese culture events are happening all the time. I strongly believe that the *Natsu-Matsuri* was a pioneer project in promoting Japanese culture and became a prototype for various Japan festivals thereafter.

Bernard Leach

In 1978 I had the opportunity to take photographs of Bernard Leach in St Ives, Cornwall. He established the Leach pottery with the Japanese potter Shoji Hamada in St Ives in1920. He was well known in Japan, more than in the UK, and I wanted to meet him. He was ninety-one years old and was already blind. When I made an appointment to interview him, I suggested to Mr. K. Nakamura, the *Mainichi Shimbun* correspondent here, that he go with me so that he could write about Leach for his newspaper.

Bernard Leach was living in a maisonette overlooking Porthmeor Beach. When we arrived, he was sitting in the lounge upstairs. Through the windows we could see the sea and the white sandy beach with a few rocks scattered around here and there. Leach said, "Look out the window. Can you see black rocks there?" I said "Yes". "Do they remind you of Ryoanji temple?" he asked. Leach could not see it, but he remembered it very well, clearly imprinted on his mind. Leach talked a lot and he was very philosophical. His memory was sharp. He said Japan was the teacher of his work. He went to Japan as an etching teacher and met a potter, the sixth generation of Ogata Kenzan, at a *raku* pottery party. He was lured by the pottery, particularly *raku*, and recalled how fascinating it was at that time. Leach went on to become the seventh generation in the Kenzan pottery tradition.

During my interview in the afternoon Leach said, "Let's have tea. If you go downstairs to the fridge, there's ice cream in it. Can you bring it up? And also can you go and get muffins from the local shop?" I went downstairs and opened the fridge. I found four ceramic bowls made by him with beautiful green *matcha* ice cream in them. We also bought muffins, and we had muffins, ice cream and tea. Towards the end of the interview he asked me, "Do you have any more questions?" Actually I had run out of questions by that time! So he said, "Come back again tomorrow and talk a bit more." Obviously he liked talking and seemed to be very happy to meet Japanese people.

Shoji Hamada had died a year before, and his widow had sent Leach a letter replying to his condolence letter. Her letter was all in Japanese. Leach had a secretary called Trudy Scott but she couldn't read Japanese and he couldn't see the letter. There was no Japanese person around him either. He asked me to read the letter for him. So I read Shoji Hamada's wife's letter to him, and that was the first time he found out the contents of the letter. He started crying. It was a very emotional moment.

Bernard Leach died in 1979, within a year of my photographing him. My photographs of Bernard Leach became the last photographs of him. I wrote an obituary for a Japanese pottery magazine. According to Shoji Hamada's widow's letter, when Shoji Hamada died he was surrounded by his children and grandchildren by the bedside and died very peacefully. On the day Bernard Leach died in the care home, there were no family members beside him, though he died peacefully. His third wife had left him, and his children and grandchildren were not present either. I thought it was very sad, but it is an English way in a sense. The Japanese always live surrounded by family, but the English live more independently and have an individual way. He was of the Ba'hai religion and buried in St Ives in a church cemetery. But his grave is not in the Christian section of the cemetery, it is at the very far end of the cemetery and we could recognise it only with a small black stone memorial. I felt sorry, but that must have been as he wished.

The Leach Pottery Restoration Project

After Bernard Leach's wife Janet died in 1997, the Leach Pottery in St Ives in Cornwall became very run-down and local people set up a restoration project. I joined the project as the Japan liaison officer in 2004. It was a very difficult job to raise funds and also to publicise it in St Ives. The director of the restoration project, Lady Carol Holland, had a meeting informing local people that we would set up the restoration project of the Leach Pottery, and asking them for their support. And a lot of local people asked, "Who is Bernard Leach?" It suggested this campaign was not going to be an easy one.

Bernard Leach was, on the contrary, well known in Japan. Back in Japan, first I went to meet the *Asahi Shimbun* art editor. I talked to him about the project and he took an interest in what I said. He asked me to write an article about it which he would publish in the national paper. I explained the project and asked readers of the *Asahi Shimbun* to send supporting e-mails to the Leach Pottery. On the day that my article was published, more than a hundred e-mails arrived at the project office from Japan. Carol was so surprised but very encouraged. I was impressed by the *Asahi Shimbun's* power and also by Bernard Leach's popularity in Japan. That was the beginning of my campaign in Japan.

Then I went to the *Mingei-kan* (folk museum) and met a lady called Taeko Utsumi who was head of the international section. She was Soetsu Yanagi's friend and through him knew Bernard Leach. She was interested in the project and decided to help. And then I went to Mashiko and met Hamada's grandson, Tomoo Hamada, and he was very co-operative and promised to help.

I knew the then Japanese Ambassador in London, Mr Yoshiji Nogami. I spoke to him about the project and asked the Embassy to help. He was very helpful and agreed to visit the Leach Pottery and to become a patron of the project. That summer I received a telephone call from Toyoko Fry, the Japanese wife of Graham Fry, the British Ambassador in Japan. She said, "We're going to St Ives and would like to visit the Leach Pottery." I asked Carol and other committee members of the project to greet them and also I asked if the British Ambassador would like to join the project as a patron. I was so glad that I could manage to bring on board the Japanese media, Japanese and British Ambassadors as patrons, the Minegei-kan and Mashiko to the Leach project.

Ambassador Fry held a big presentation reception at the British Embassy in Tokyo inviting the Japanese press and television, gallery owners and influential people to launch the Leach Pottery Restoration Project, and I was invited to give a presentation. Ambassador Nogami organised a one-day seminar on Bernard Leach at the Japanese Embassy in London together with the exhibition of my photographs of Bernard Leach in the Embassy gallery.

With an enormous effort by the British restoration project team chaired by Carol Holland and the contribution from the Japanese side, the Leach Pottery was successfully restored and opened to the public in 2009. We managed to bring Tomoo Hamada, grandson of Shoji Hamada, and John Leach, grandson of Bernard Leach, together to cut a tape for the opening ceremony. The Leach Pottery project is still going on and now it's an international pottery centre with Japanese and other potters having residencies from time to time. It trains apprentices to make standard ware and St Ives has become an official "Friendly City" with Mashiko. The Japanese Embassy in London held a reception for that, and the Crafts Council organised a London craft fair and Mashiko potters took part in it.

Promoting cultural understanding

I think the important role I am able to play here is in a liaison capacity with Japan and Britain at the grassroots level. It's mainly in the fields of culture and life-style. I am always interested in the different life-styles and the different sense of value each country has. Japan and Britain are very similar but at the same time are quite different. They need to understand each other more and I am always working on that.

In fact I am spending more time on making the Japanese people understand British culture than making the British understand Japanese culture. There are over 60,000 Japanese people living in the UK, but 80 per cent of them are in transit. They are mostly businessmen, their families and students, and they are here for only two to four years. They enjoy going to theatres and concerts and visiting Europe on holidays. The recent economic recession in Japan has overshadowed the Japanese community here, too. The number of Japanese businessmen and students has slightly dropped, but still there is a quite big Japanese community here. I think it is a pity if you came and stayed here for three years but went back to Japan without experiencing the British life style or the British sense of values. It is often the case that Japanese people living here never make a British friend, or they hardly have any chance to speak English. I think that's my job, through my publications, articles and photographs, to show how the British systems work and how the British people think and behave.

Looking to the future

I've got over three hundred thousand photographs. Jill asked, if I die, what would she do with all these negatives and transparencies? I know I have to sort out all the photographs one day. Most photographs were taken on my assignments for Japanese magazines and have mostly been used once already. But some of them are historically very important and should be carefully categorised. I've displayed some of my 1970s photographs at a Japanese pub in Chancery Lane in London. Photographers never retire, so I'm always carrying a camera and new photographs are added to my collection all the time. It is rather difficult to sort out the past while you are still working.

Until recently I had been contributing a photo essay series to the Yomiuri Shimbun for the last 10 years. I introduced one photograph with an essay every week showing different aspects of Britain. The series was called "The Faces of Britain", and I had done more than three hundred aspects. Also I edit the Nippon Club's newsletter. For that, I write, take photographs, edit and do layout. Literally I do everything myself.

Also I teach photography now. I have about twenty Japanese adult students. We meet in a Japanese restaurant once a month. I set a monthly theme and students are required to take photos on the theme and bring them to the next meeting for the assessment. The standard of photographs by the students is now quite high, and a bi-monthly Japanese magazine called 'Euro News' commissioned us to supply photographs for the front cover of each issue. So the students are delighted to get their picture published each month, and get paid!

I love England of course, and I also love Japan. A lot of people ask me whether I would go back to Japan when I retire. The problem is that you only have one body. You cannot be in two different places at the same time. I feel that the two countries are my two mistresses. It is rather difficult to say a good-bye to either of them. If you really want to know which I prefer, I would say, "Maybe here."

I have been here more than half of my life now. I don't think I would go back to Japan to live. If I did, I would have to start again and I'm a bit too old to do that. We have a house in London and a small hideaway in Devon. My parents have long gone, but I have a sister in Tokyo. She is now in an old people's home, and I often go back to Japan to see her. I have many Japanese friends; they are university friends, photographer and journalist friends, and friends I made while they were in London. I feel now I have one leg in Britain and the other leg in Japan. Both legs are deeply rooted in the ground and it's rather difficult to pull one leg out.

Both Jill and I are freelance and don't have a retirement age. We think we will carry on working until the time comes when we cannot physically carry on anymore. However I know I can't carry on forever. I'm over seventy years old now and have to think of a retirement life. I might be growing Japanese vegetables, sorting out all the photographs and writing books. However, nothing is realistic yet – I am still too busy with today's appointment, tomorrow's deadlines, and attending the Japanese Embassy's receptions.

SETSUO KATO

Photo-Journalist, Publisher, Archivist for the Japanese Community in the UK

	Born in Tokyo
1962-66	Studied journalism at Waseda University, Tokyo
1966	Joined Keystone Press Agency in Tokyo
1970	Came to London to study photo journalism at College of Journalism in Fleet Street; met Jill Fanshawe, British ceramicist, married in Tokyo in 1974
1977	Settled in London as a resident with Jill; published numerous articles on British life for the Japanese media including newspapers, magazines, radio and television
1978	Photographed Bernard Leach and published article in *Weekly Post* 1979
1983-	Editor of the London Nippon Club's official newsletter *Big Ben* – ongoing
1985-90	Founded the Anglo-Japanese Summer Festival held in Battersea Park, an annual festival of Japanese music, dance, entertainments and food stalls attracting over 3,000 people
1991	Started publishing *Nichi-Ei Times* for Japanese residents in the UK – ended in 2002
2004-08	Worked to promote the Bernard Leach Pottery Restoration Project in St. Ives, Cornwall, acting as fund-raiser, publicist and liaison officer with Japanese institutions and potters, culminating in a grand opening ceremony in 2008
2008-10	Set up the Japanese Garden Restoration Project in Hammersmith Park, London, to restore the historic garden created for the Great Japan-British Exhibition of 1910; became Director ofthe Japan-British Exhibition 100 Committee to oversee restoration of the garden in time for the centenary commemoration in 2010

2015   Continues to work as a photographer and editor, and
            support the Japanese community in the UK

AWARDS

2000   Awarded Japanese Ambassador's Award for services
            to the Japanese community

2000   The Japan Society Award for services to Japan/UK
            relations

2015   Received the Japanese Foreign Minister's
            commendation for contributing and promoting Anglo-
            Japanese relations and helping the Japanese
            Community in the UK

DIRECTORSHIPS & MEMBERSHIPS

            Director of the Japan-British Exhibition 100 Committee

            Permanent Membership of the Leach Pottery
            Foundation

            Member of National Union of Journalists

            General Committee of Nippon Club

            Establishing Member of the Japanese Residents Assoc
            in UK – now The Japan Association

            Editor of Nippon Club Newsletter Liaison Officer of
            Leach Pottery Preservation Project

            Japan Society Award Selection Committee

            Director of Ichiza Theatre Co. – Japanese theatre
            company in the UK

            Director of Azuki Foundation – charity promoting
            Japanese culture in the UK

LIBRARY ARCHIVES

            All copies of the *Nichi-Ei Times'* are stored in the
            following archives:

            The British Library

            The Japanese National Diet Library

            The Japan Society Library

            The Embassy of Japan, London Library

The Nichi-Ei Times 1991-2002, and other books by Setsuo Kato

PROFESSOR TOSHIO WATANABE

HISTORIAN IN ANGLO-JAPANESE CROSS-CULTURAL STUDIES, ART & DESIGN

"Suddenly I made a Korean joke. "Oh my god, I did a racist joke!"
So 'I'm a good boy, I'm a mixed blood, so I'm not a racist!'

"It's an assumption, and suddenly I realised I'm part of the cultural
product of that particular milieu; so now I always say, "I'm a racist – but
I try and control it." But almost everybody is a racist, because everybody
is a product of the culture which has a hierarchical view of others."

Professor Toshio Watanabe

The 'Peace Child'

My father is Japanese, my mother German. I was born in Switzerland and my Japanese great-grandfather was a Major-General who participated in the Russo-Japanese War of 1904-05. My great-uncle, Watanabe Setsu, is quite a well-known architect; he designed the Kyoto station in the Taisho period, which created a furore. At Tokyo station the central door is always closed because it's for the Emperor. But Watanabe Setsu thought that was a waste of space, so he reserved the central entrance for everybody, and put the Emperor's entrance at the side. Somehow he got away with it! In the family he's known as a despot and a tyrant, but he was a well-known person at the time.

My father, Mamoru grew up with his grandparents, and went to *Gakushuin* primary school, where he was the only *heimin* – non-aristocratic person – in the class. My father graduated from Tokyo University, then got a scholarship to study in Germany, going there in 1938. All his wealth was kept in cash in banks, and so he basically lost everything after the War. During the War he met my mother in Vienna, while he was teaching at the Japanology Department. He said there was only about a dozen Japanese in the whole of Vienna, and that the musical life was fantastic. Actually aesthetics was his main subject, but because of the great music life in Vienna while he was there during the War, he became a musicologist; later became a prominent figure in Japan, and eventually became a professor at Tokyo University's Aesthetics Department. He was also a very good writer, and became a regular radio presenter with his own classical music programme for NHK Radio 2, like BBC Radio 3. So he was a well-known voice, and became a Wagner specialist in Japan.

My great-great-grandfather on my mother's side was the head gardener of *Schönbrunn* Palace in Vienna. After his death the family moved to Silesia. Then my grandmother went to Transylvania in Romania and married my grandfather, also a German, owner of an electrical goods shop and also a wildlife officer employed by the city. Transylvanian cities were basically built by Germans in medieval times and my mother was born in *Kronstadt* which is now called *Brasov*; I've no relatives left there. My mother, who was very good with languages, decided she wanted to study some exotic language, and my grandmother suggested Japanese half-jokingly, and she thought it was a great idea! So she went to Vienna to study Japanese. My mother said that she cried all the way on the train from Romania to Vienna, but didn't know why. And later she knew – because that was the last time she saw her father. The War came and the Iron Curtain came down, she couldn't go back; and there was a complete loss of connection. Only after she got married and had two children, my sister and I, both born in Switzerland, was she able to reconnect with her family thanks to the Red Cross.

My mother and father met in Vienna, and they wanted to marry, but they were not allowed to do so, because although Japan was not an enemy they were sort of 'alien'. My mother only confessed shortly before she died that actually I already existed before they got married in Switzerland. My father went first to Switzerland because it was a neutral country and found a really boring job, transcribing deciphered messages, so at least he had a clerk's job in the Embassy in Bern. He wanted my mother to join him and she took one of the last trains to that particular border town. She got the ticket and was queuing but because she was pregnant some kind people said, 'Look, there's a bench over there, we'll keep your place, just sit there...' and as she was resting there, an official came and put a tape between her and the queue and said only people on her side could go on the train. And all the nice people couldn't get on the train! She said it was thanks to me that she could join my father.

So my parents got married in Bern and the most dramatic bit of my autobiography is my birth in August 1945. 6th of August was Hiroshima, 9th of August was Nagasaki, and because Switzerland was neutral a telegram came from Japan asking the Japanese Embassy to negotiate whether there was any possibility for a conditional surrender; obviously they realised that this was the end. So all the Embassy staff were working very hard on August 10th, and my father came back in the evening to the hospital, and at shortly before 7pm I was born. So I'm the 'Peace Child' because I was born on 10th August, and 15th August was the end of the war with the Emperor's Proclamation.

Early days in Japan

My national identity is Japanese, because I grew up there. I have no memory of Switzerland, and the first memory is of Japan. My passport is Japanese, and that's it. When I got married I needed a birth certificate, a passport isn't enough, and I just couldn't find the original. So I actually wrote to the Lutheran Church in Berne and asked for another copy of the birth certificate. I got a really nice letter back because the current priest there consulted the retired priest who actually baptised me, and he remembered such an unusual baby! I thought that was lovely, that he remembered!

At home we spoke German as well as Japanese. My father spoke very fluent German, he spoke also some English, some Italian, some French and some Bulgarian; but my mother was probably the better linguist, and her Japanese was quite good. Once I moved back to Europe as an adult, they came over more or less every summer. The funny thing was that we would talk in German, and it would be my mother who broke into Japanese first, without realising that she was doing it!

Anyway, when I was a baby we had to leave Switzerland. Indonesia was in the war zone so we had to take a ship from Genoa, through the Panama Canal and up to San Francisco, then travel by another ship to Japan. My mother found this really hard, as she was discriminated against as a 'traitor white woman' for marrying a Japanese. When we arrived in Japan, my father had no job and no money, and we stayed in a hospital run by a relative, living in a patient's room. I must have been about two or three years old and remember the kitchen, because in Japan at the time it was the family's obligation to look after the patient, not necessarily the nurse's. And there was this big kitchen with all these mothers and wives, and I still remember it was very large, and this din of the women going *"Warawarawara!"* and the steam...

But obviously it was quite difficult for my parents, and my mother somehow got the idea to publish a knitwear book. It was in 1948, just one year after they came back. The publisher, called 'Ondorisha' – *ondori* is a cockerel specialised in knitwear publications, patterns, books and 'how to' kind of books (it went bankrupt only recently). My mother became a famous knitwear designer and her number one pupil, Ito Hiroko – who is now over eighty – had an exhibition recently in Tokyo which she does every two years. The first time that my sister and I went to one of these exhibitions was four years ago. It was really very emotional, and then I thought that, 'Ah, this may be a chance to do an interview,' finding out what kind of teacher my mother was. Ito Hiroko is also the knitting teacher of Empress Michiko! How high can you go? She's obviously from a very good family; she said her father was high up in TEPCO, Tokyo Electric Power Company. She got into knitwear when she was seventeen and her mother saw this first volume of knitwear, and thought, "This is brilliant!" So she simply went to my mother and said, "Can you teach my daughter?" There are only two other people from that generation still alive. And I interviewed both of them, it was amazing; I was thinking, "I'm also a design historian, why didn't I think of doing it before?"

Experiencing comparative cultures

My main interest as a scholar is 'transnational art' and what it means, and I always wanted to do comparative culture. There are certain moments in my school life which were, retrospectively, very useful for me. The first incident was at a Jesuit boys' school, where I think I was the only mixed blood person in the class. While we were playing – as part of the fight – one of the pupils said, "Well, your blood is not pure! You are mixed, you're not pure Japanese!" Wow! But before I could do anything, all the others pounced on him, "You can't say that!" And so I didn't have to do anything! So I won! I thought that was really a lovely experience for me.

Very often, even close friends forget that I look even exotic; when young I looked more exotic than now. But then another really life-changing experience happened while I was in upper high school and suddenly without thinking I made a Korean joke, "Oh my God, I did a racist joke!" This was like cold water pouring over me, because there is this arrogance of being mixed blood. Western-looking was fashionable, and other people thought I was good-looking, and I got attention from the girls and so on. It is actually not a great thing, as I thought, 'I'm a good boy, because I'm a mixed blood, so I'm not a racist!' It's a stupid assumption, and suddenly I realised I'm part of the cultural product of that particular milieu. Each milieu has its own racial hierarchy. And without realising, I was part of that, so therefore, now I always say, "I'm a racist – but I try to control it." But also, more or less everybody is a racist, because everybody is a product of the culture which has a hierarchical view of others. I think that was quite an important experience for me, and also really put me into place; that was the important thing.

Another life-changing experience came when I was a teenager in high school. I was at home, where my room was next to my parents', but it was just a wooden, sliding door, so the soundproofing wasn't great. One day my parents were having a quarrel, and suddenly a 'eureka' lamp went up in me, because I realised my mother couldn't understand my father's argument; and my father couldn't understand my mother's argument. But I could understand both sides of the argument; I could understand my mother's, what she was saying, and I could also understand my father's, what he was saying, so I thought I have to make this understanding my vocation.

University life

Because I had been in a Jesuit high school I could actually get into Sophia University without the normal entrance examination. I had to get at least a certain level, because *Eiko Gakuen,* which was the school name, was one of the really top private schools when it came to sending pupils to Tokyo University. I actually wanted to do something in music, because I love music. I used to play clarinet in a brass band, and also conducted it. At Sophia University I ran the university orchestra. Then my father said, "Probably it's better, if you really want to enjoy music, not to make it a profession." As the perpetual second clarinet, at least I had enough insight to know that whoever was the first clarinet played better. Also I had a problem with the study of harmony, so I thought music wasn't my career.

I realised very quickly that I was not a scientist, so I needed to brush up my German. I saw that was my expertise very few people had. My German was very fluent, but faulty, so I thought I really had to sort it out. I went to Sophia University's German

Department, which probably had the highest reputation in this subject. I was doing German studies but was rather lazy in my studies, because I was involved with the orchestra club and falling in love, which was very exciting! My first university year was 1964, which was of course the year of the Tokyo Olympics, and I was doing an interpreter job for the German department. That was real field training, so I didn't have to go to classes. For the entire period of the Olympics I was an interpreter for German television and it was so exciting!

1964 – A key year of change for Japan

I think 1964 was the first time when Japan became a more positive place, now the post-War period and the post-War misery was *over*. Just a few years after the return to Japan, our family moved from Tokyo to Hayama at the coast, a beautiful small town with a great view of Mt Fuji over the sea on a clear day. We were still not well-off, but once a month or so we went to *Zushi* to have a bowl of *ramen*, which was great! You see in the 1950s black and white films that actually the street scenes in Japan were extremely modest, and people lived very modestly. The Japanese prosperity really could be felt only after 1964.

Recently I read an interesting article by Watanabe Hiroshi (no relation) about the highways in Tokyo. Now many people regard them as a blot on the scenery. But that article said it was actually a sign of modernity at the time, and it was also regarded as beautiful, all this sinuous line across the city. Then the Bullet train [*Shinkansen*] came in, and also Kenzo Tange's Olympic buildings. I interviewed him at the time, and he was really great, very straightforward and a good interviewee. The *Kasumigaseki* building was the first skyscraper in Tokyo with 36 floors. Before that the height restriction was there because, if you built too high, you could look down to the Emperor. That's why in Marunouchi in Tokyo facing the palace all the buildings were the same height, with the beautiful view of the moat next to the Imperial Plaza. The German interviewer asked Tange, "But can't you build a hundred, or two hundred floor building?" and Tange said, "Yes, that's still safe, but with earthquakes you will get seasick on the top floor!" And he explained why, in a very simple way. That's really when post-War Japan came into hi-tech modernity, in 1964.

Usually as a historian, you are very doubtful about highlighting a specific date. Things don't change that radically from one year to the other and there are lots of criticisms even about highlighting 1945. For example, there was a group of art historians who looked at 1940s art; the first half and second half, to see it as a single unit. Also the year 1868 is often seen when something completely feudal suddenly changed into something all so modern, but most historians now see it as a transitional period. I like that, but for me as this youngster, the changes of 1964 felt sudden, life changing, and full of hope.

The golden period of art historians

The first two years of my university life were so easy, because I could already speak German! And all the teachers thought I spoke it well, so gave good marks. Then in the third year Shinoda-sensei walked in. Professor Shinoda Yujiro was an expert on Labour Law I think, and was also a consultant to Toyota. But he did his PhD on Art History in Cologne on Degas and Japan. At times he appeared rather arrogant as a person, but he was extremely fluent in German. He walked into this compulsory class on German cultural history, and gave his lecture in machine-gun German with no concession to the abilities of the students in front. He gave his lecture and then just left. It was a total shock for me because I thought for me German was no problem, but I could only understand about one third of what he was saying! He didn't explain any jargon or anything; and obviously all the other classmates were also in shock. I thought, "Dammit, I must find out what this is about!" That lecture gave me the first motivation to learn seriously.

His lack of concession to our ability really stimulated me and I found art history very interesting. I came to it quite late, as Sophia University didn't have any postgraduate possibilities for doing art history. Then I heard that Tokyo University had this system called *Gakushi nyugaku* which is where somebody who already has a B.A. can go straight to the third year of Tokyo University's four year B.A. degree. I got in and I read Art History there. It was actually a 'golden period' of the great art historians. Professors Yoshikawa Itsuji, Yamane Yuzo, Suzuki Kei etc., etc. I could see the standard was high. Among them was Professor Akiyama Terukazu, the greatest scholar of the *Heian* period scroll paintings, and by chance his secretary was related to my family. Also my father was at the Tokyo University as Aesthetics Professor and they knew each other very well. I went to him for advice because Professor Akiyama was Professor of Comparative Culture, and he said, "No, you shouldn't specialise in Comparative Culture to start with, but should specialise in either East Asian art, Japanese art, or Western art. And if you want postgraduate studies, then you can start comparing, because you need one firm field you really know about otherwise it becomes superficial." So I chose Western art history because I had my German, I lived in Western countries, so in my environment that was a natural choice.

1968 students' revolts

1968 was the great year for student revolts. For six months it was peaceful and then it wasn't any more, it was the biggest student revolt in Japanese history, and its greatest focal point was Tokyo University. Towards the end it went so bad that the main auditorium was occupied by the Left Radicals who went in and barricaded themselves in with concrete. The entire media was on it, 24 hours a day, so the police could not do something really brutal. They even tried to use helicopters, but every day people were watching it on television.

I was what's called 'non-poli' – non-political – but it was also that time when I really learned my 'lessons of life' in a sense that you just have to find out what you can believe, and then act according to your beliefs, but also continue to listen to the others and try to understand them. I went around to all the groupings, the Communists, the Anti-Communist Radicals and the right wing ones. The group I hated most at the time were the Communists; they were extremely powerful, extremely well organised, they all wore anoraks, and their march was splendid, a really good march. But they were completely under the hand of the Communist Party, so I felt, as a youngster, they were just like lackeys, they had no freedom to say 'no' to the bosses. But they were very powerful. The most attractive ones were actually the left radicals, the anti-communists, they were really idealists, and they were extremely eloquent, but they also looked a bit mad and not always open to logic, and towards the end they had factionalised so much, they became very violent.

Meeting Mishima Yukio

A friend from school said, 'Somebody wants to meet a Tokyo University student, do you want to come?' It was the writer Mishima Yukio, and I said, "Okay, okay!" a fantastic invitation! So I went to a club somewhere in Aoyama. There were only about five of us I remember, and there were Mishima Yukio and Agawa Hiroyuki, another novelist, and it was an experience! Mishima was tiny but so polite; his speech was very gentle, almost feminine, basically he spoke like a man from a good family, which he was. I thought he was a straight talker. Whereas Agawa Hiroyuki... I didn't know why Mishima went around with Agawa, because he started to boast about his war experience, knowing that Mishima couldn't because he didn't survive the physical checkup. Mishima was also muscly, but – his *eyes*! He really had those penetrating, fantastic eyes! He was interested in the whole Tokyo University student revolt thing. Also then the Faculty of Literature students voted to strike. I found my document, the brochure of that time, and I had written in how many voted; and there were over 70% of the students present. I voted against, but overwhelmingly they voted to strike, so it was democratically decided therefore I respected that.

There was one memorable moment for me when the Tokyo University issue became the focus of the nation. There was a huge gathering of communist sympathizers, I think there were about seven thousand, all descended from different universities. And then there were left radicals, and there was a rumour that the left radicals would come to Tokyo University and attack the communists, and also occupy the faculty. About three thousand of us 'non-polis' did a sit-in between them, and also to protect the building from occupation. There was a particularly famous group, *Kakumaru*, the anti-communist left radicals from Nippon University who marched into our campus. I was sitting at the front of the human barricade. The marchers could see that they were outnumbered, but running alongside the picketing, they started to bash us with their placards. I was lucky as I was too close to them and escaped injury. A week later I appeared in a weekly magazine at the centre of a double-spread photo, shouting!

Usually people are either committed to some really radical politics or the non-committed ones are just simply 'wishy-washers', but three thousand people came who were none of these. There was also one tutor who tried to go between the attackers and the picketing students. But it was also interesting in hindsight that a really famous politics professor, Maruyama Masao, was quite unpopular among students. A number of us thought he didn't respond to the situation properly for what was happening then, though he was very good at analysis of past things. That was also an interesting thing, that as a scholar you can be a fantastic analyst, but actually if you are faced yourself with something dangerous, you don't know how best to act. It's like some persecuted scholars facing the dilemma, "Should I just die for my beliefs? Or say something wishy-washy and survive?" It's also not for me to judge, but it gave me life lessons so if, say, I got attacked and died, at least I died in peace with myself. But also I can see that these are extremely fluid situations. It sounds like bragging, but at the time it was just simply well meaning hot-headedness. This experience also helped me later when I was asked to become the branch secretary of our college staff union. I am not a Marxist and not even a socialist, but I accepted this post and, particularly in the many case works in which I was involved, my early experience helped me a lot by trying to see that justice is very important; but often how one should go forward in a productive way in life could be a little bit of sacrifice in one's own rightful claim (but not of others).

Research Centre for Transnational Art, Identity and Nation (TrAIN)

In the past I have examined the cross flow of culture between Britain and Japan during the period of the 1860s and 1930s in two large international exhibition projects. One of the key issues was how power relationships between nations impacted on their cultural relationships. It's really what the Research Centre (TrAIN) is about. I have written a very short piece on how Edward Said's 'Orientalism' as that of Western domination over the Orient, works as a formula. It's a cultural pattern which does exist, for example my colleague Kikuchi Yuko applied it to the *Mingei* (Folk Crafts Movement), and examined how Yanagi dealt with Korea, so there's an Oriental *'Orientalism'* as well. As a formula you can apply it, but it is important to see that this is not the whole story. Said has been criticised about this, but in his later writings, he took up a more nuanced position. The later debate on the hybridity by Homi Bhabha extended this discussion on "What is East, and what is West?" A lot of what we think of as West actually consists of a lot of East, it gets blurred! That's why I'm interested in the transnational, the border territory, that's where all the exciting things happen. So in 2004 I set up with my colleagues the Research Centre for Transnational Art, Identity and Nation (TrAIN). The notion of 'transnational' was not a very common term then and people kept asking me what it meant. At the time when I googled it, TrAIN always came on top. For me the one term definition of what is transnational is 'messy'.

Basically, it's about porous borders. It doesn't mean that the concept 'East and West' doesn't exist, but it's just that the border between them is so porous. Also the definition is 'beyond national'. In art history most artists are talked about in national terms; the Olympics are the same, football is the same. The 'national' still has a very heavy identity issue, and then for lots of people it's important for them. Like Japanese artists, British artists, it confirms their own identity. Very often 'international' has two meanings; one is something which is not national, like 'international waters', which no nation has claim to, or it's gathering point for lots of nationals like the United Nations, which is an international organisation where lots of nationals are represented together. So 'transnational' is all sort of much more fuzzy things, also the word itself has no sense of hierarchy, that's what I like about it.

The word did exist, but wasn't that common, and now it's very common in cultural history and so on. Also, the whole world is part of a globalisation, though I tend not to use 'globalisation' because it gives a more homogenising feel; everything is not the same across the globe. Everyone has a different kind of identity or even identities, and any identity is not fixed. It is perpetually changing and is fluid. Once you recognise this, you can see that it's so fascinating. Fixed and rigid identity will at closer scrutiny become more varied and fluid. Let's look at Japan. It always had transnationalism and to see Japanese traditional culture as something 'pure' and unchanging is rubbish. For example, I'm so grateful for these great Mongolian *Yokozunas* in Sumo wrestling, because without the Mongolians this most traditional sport of Japan would be nowhere. The Mongolian *Hakuho* is the greatest living Sumo wrestler, regardless of nationality, and may become even the greatest in Sumo history.

Japonisme and Orientalism

I'm interested in aspects of Japonisme, which we may define as 'a taste for things Japanese'. This phenomenon is part of a long tradition of the Western yearning for an ideal East. It even goes back to the classic legend of El Dorado, the golden island in the East, and European culture has had that tradition since then. It's the Utopia you don't have, whatever kind of things you like, but it's a construct. Each period had its own representative Eastern culture for this orientalism [not in the sense of Said]. For the eighteenth century it was the dreamy land of imaginary Cathay and from the mid-nineteenth century Japan took over the role of the representative Oriental culture for the West. Particularly for the British this partly came about as the image of the two previously idealized Eastern cultures, China and India, got tainted through the Opium Wars in China and the Great Rebellion of 1857 in India. And suddenly out of nowhere up pops Japan, which seems to be governed by an aesthetic, perfect life. Many western travellers went first to China and then to Japan and during the nineteenth century there was more or less a unanimity of opinion that China was dirty, Japan was clean, China was gaudy and Japan wa sophisticated, etc. Japan took over as the idealised East from China.

Post Modernism and Modernity

Once we get into the twentieth century we have a much more complicated and varied response to the East including to China and Japan. What I also wanted to investigate was not only how the West looked at Japan, but also how did Japan's response to modernity compare with others. Well, everybody does struggle with modernity, and how did other non-Euro-American cultures face this issue? We got funding for a research project called 'Modernity and National Identity in Art: India, Japan, Mexico, 1860s-1930s'. Sounds rather crazy to have these three nations together. We had three groups of about seven scholars for each country. Basically the point was not to find a connection between those three countries, but to find whether there were any similarities or differences in how each dealt with the issue of modernity. All three are in one way peripheral cultures, from the Western point of view. But each of them had to face their own modernity, and how the artists responded to the condition of modernity in each of those countries was the thing we looked at. It was a fabulous project. I really loved it, because I could also ask these sorts of idiot questions to, say, the Mexico group, "What is Mestizaje?" and they had to explain it to us non-experts in a clear and understandable way. That was really lovely and actually we did a conference at the V&A in 1996 and I managed to get as the keynote speaker Homi Bhabha from Chicago!

Post Modernism is also in one way a variation of modernism, and what is modernity? There are various things like the urban condition, expanded media, ease of communication and transport, nature as place for leisure activities etc. All these are abstract concepts, but Mexico City has it, Tokyo has it, Shanghai has it, New York has it and so on. For the big urban cultures that sort of issue of modernity is now shared, but also in each place there are slightly different issues, and each has to deal with it in their own way. Art, history, sports and so on are so much governed by nation, but in reality a lot of things aren't. For example, in Japan some of the most popular TV programmes are Korean soaps. My sister is a real devotee and has the entire series of the *Fuyu Sona* 'Winter Sonata', and she sent me a set of DVDs, but I'm so afraid to start watching it! Another art historian I know got sucked in because his wife was watching, and then he couldn't get out of this! And they've become so addictive, because if you look at the details, what you think is national, very often it isn't. Japan had an uneasy relationship with Korea and it seems it is getting worse, but still they love watching these Korean soaps. This is an example where cultural consumption becomes transnational, i.e. transcending the national.

A question of identity

The Japanese have a strong sense of identity, but what that is can be quite strange. A few years ago I attended a design conference at the Royal Society of Arts, and it was on Design Branding – again the identity issue – and the marketing manager of British Airways gave a most fascinating talk. He said, though sometimes it's shortened to BA, they still insist on calling it British Airways, because the 'British' is the brand, which is a different thing from the other airlines. So when they're making TV advertisements all over the world, that's their selling point. But what he said is that, 'What they think is typically British is different from country to country.' What Japanese think is typically British is different from what Americans think. So the marketing manager has to find out what are the British stereotypes perceived in each country, and adjust his adverts. I thought that was fascinating. The same applies also in reverse, say, with the Japanese, what each Japanese thinks is typically Japanese is probably different to what another Japanese thinks is typical. What is Japan now could be manga, J-Pop, anime etc.

Japan, China and South Korea

Japan's relations with its near neighbours, China and South Korea, is very interesting for me now, because for my generation in Japan, they were the most alien places, as we just didn't talk about them. Anyway the culture we studied was their old culture. I loved Tang poetry, but was completely incurious of what was going on in contemporary Chinese poetry. Also travel restrictions out of Japan were only lifted in 1968, as late as that. Complete freedom was restricted, because you had to get permission to buy foreign currency, and there was an upper limit. Also you had to give reasons why you were travelling. By 1964 the reason for travel could be tourism albeit with this financial restriction, but after 1968 it was completely free. The first time I went out to Europe was I think 1965 and I was actually part of a group of Sophia University's German study group at the Freiburg University language course. I completely ignored it and travelled around hitchhiking, it was lovely. Because I was doing Western art, and by background am half-German, my eyes were just focused on Europe, then finally I could go, but Asia didn't come into it. More recently my curiosity on the relationship of Japanese art with China, India or Korea has been stimulated and I am trying to catch up lost ground.

I'm also interested in the first half of the 20th century's relationship with China and Japan, which was very close. Lots of Chinese came to study in Japan, but previously for the Communist China to acknowledge that the Chinese could have benefited from Japanese education was taboo except for Lu Xun, the famous writer, as everybody knows that he went to Japan, and that was okay just for this one case. The Tokyo School of Fine Arts trained many of the Chinese artists who went back and set up art academies in China. Now the taboo has begun to loosen, so there's really much more exciting research on that period by the younger scholars on both sides and also in North America, so there is lots of interesting stuff that is coming out. It was a very close relationship; again it's completely transnational.

Forgotten Japonisme

Another project I got involved with was called ' Forgotten Japonisme: Taste for Japanese Art in Britain and USA 1920s-1950s', which strongly focused on the first half of the twentieth century. The classic Japonisme of impressionism, etc. petered out during the early twentieth century and from the 1964 Tokyo Olympics onwards we have the hi-tech Japonisme of the Bullet train, Sony Walkman, etc. What happened in between? We had no formal external collaborators and all the investigators were TrAIN members. Therefore the entire half million pounds funding came into our university coffers. We gained a lot of internal kudos. This was another highly enjoyable project. Our conclusions were in short that there was no break in the taste for Japanese things even during the war period. Even in the USA after Pearl Harbor, Americans were buying Japanese artworks, which is evidenced by auction catalogues. But we also questioned Japanese taste for whom? Many Japanese gardens in North America were created by Japanese-Americans and represented their identity. Japonisme could surely not be only the preserve of white Caucasians?

Japanese gardens and future projects

One of my next projects – hopefully I'll get the funding – is Japanese gardens and World War Two. One of the things I found out once I got interested in modern Japanese garden is there's been very little done on colonial Japanese gardens. There must be hundreds, if not thousands, of Japanese gardens in Asia; they'll be in Taiwan and Korea and elsewhere. In the colonies, there were lots of Japanese-type houses built, and then *any* Japanese house would have a garden, however small. Also public buildings would have park-like gardens around. Why hasn't this been researched more in detail in the past? I think part of the reason is that garden historians tend to like the aesthetic value of the gardens they research. They are researching something nice, whereas Japanese colonial garden could be a rather nasty subject investigating possible Japanese cultural imperialism in Asia! I had to face the same self-reflection on why I have been doing Japonisme studies. As a Japanese scholar, Japonisme is a nice subject. You see, Western people admiring Japan! Art historians tend to pick nice and beautiful subjects, whereas sociologists tend to pick subjects as nasty as possible. I think scholars in cultural studies in art have been a good force in leveling these tendencies and I learned a lot from them.

I don't have a favourite art form; I'm a rather unusual art historian in not specialising in any medium; painting, architecture, design, popular prints, anything if it sort of fits in. My hobby is music, I used to play clarinet but don't any more, I play 'plink-plonk' piano occasionally, but listening to music, I love that, especially going to the opera. When I was a student in Japan in the 1960s, I worked as an interpreter for Osaka Festival when they got the whole of Bayreuth team over. It was just after the death of Wieland Wagner and I still remember his superb *Tristan* with Nilsson, Windgassen and Hotter, Boulez conducting. A dream ticket! That experience really hooked me into the world of opera.

I spend all my working life in art colleges, and I feel it is a privilege for an art historian to work with practitioners. In particular I have taught quite a number of fine art students at PhD level. I love particularly the early tutorials when the student has to tell me what their project is about. Sometimes they cannot articulate it clearly and it gradually emerges during the to and fro of the conversations in the tutorial. It's just such a rich kind of tapestry coming out; that's what I love. I also like to go to conferences where I meet young scholars. At the moment I feel North America has many strong mid-career historians of Japanese art and now their brilliant students are gradually emerging. We have already reached the point where all art historians in Japan have to get acquainted with these scholarships. The exciting conversations with these scholars keeps me young!

PROFESSOR TOSHIO WATANABE

Scholar, Historian in Anglo-Japanese Cross-Cultural Studies, Art and Design

	Born in Bern, Switzerland to Japanese father and German mother
1960s	Grew up in Japan, read German at Sophia University and ran the university orchestra
1964	Worked as an interpreter for German television on the Tokyo Olympics
1960s	Studied Japanese and Western art history at Tokyo University; during student riots interviewed the writer Mishima Yukio (1968)
1970s	Studied at the Courtauld Institute of Art and completed PhD at Basel University
1980s	Taught at City of Birmingham Polytechnic; ran MA course in History of Art & Design
1986	Became Head of Art History at Chelsea School of Art, then Head of Research
2000s	Director of Research Centre for Transnational Art, Identity & Nation (TrAIN) at Chelsea, now University of the Arts London (UAL)
2015	Continues to write in new fields of research, including the history of colonial Japanese gardens and World War II, and other projects

PUBLICATIONS & AWARDS

1991	*High Victorian Japonisme* – Winner of the 1992 Prize for Society for Study of Japonisme, Tokyo
1992	*Japan and Britain: An Aesthetic Dialogue: 1850-1930*
1997	*Ruskin in Japan: Nature for Art, Art for Life* – Winner of Japan Festival Prize (1998) and Gesner Gold Award (1999)

1998	Chair of the Association of Art Historians for three years
2001	Conducted three year AHRB Research Project *Modernity and National Identity in Art: India, Japan and Mexico 1860s-1940s*
2002	Member of the Tate Britain Council for three years
2005	President of Japan Art History Forum (USA) for six years
2007	Conducted three year AHRC research project on *Forgotten Japonisme: The Taste for Japanese Art in Britain & the USA 1920s-1950s*
2010	Vice President of the Comité International d'histoire de l'Art (CIHA) for six years

Ondorisha knitwear catalogue c.1948

KEIKO HOLMES OBE

FOUNDER OF AGAPE WORLD FOR POW RECONCILIATION AND HUMANITARIAN WORK

"It was almost taboo then, to speak about the war. But now we visit lots of different organisations, the POWs go to schools, visit universities, churches, so we mix with lots of people; even Buddhist people invite us, and give us accommodation.

"The first group called themselves "The Pioneers," and they met with some of their Japanese counterparts. And yes, some people apologised. Lots of people came, and wherever we go, say "Oh, the Iruka Boys!" and they apologised; "Sorry," "Gomen nasai, gomen nasai". The government and politicians are living in a different world."

Keiko Holmes OBE

A rural childhood

I was born in the countryside as the first of five children in Nishiyama village in Honshu. It is in a remote, mountainous area with spectacular scenery. When I was growing up, the village was thriving because of the copper mine located in the next village, Iruka (now known as Kiwa-Cho) about 10 miles away. The mine closed when I was away at high school, and many people left the neighbouring villages for new employment. These scattered villages amalgamated and became a town, Kiwa-Cho thus eligible for government aid. As a child, I did not appreciate living in a rural area and I longed to live in a city. Now I am grateful to go back there almost each year, where I can just be quiet and appreciate the scenery.

My father owned a civil engineering business and was always busy, and although we usually shared meals, as a family we didn't have much time together so there was little chance of relaxing and chatting with him. My mother was my father's assistant accountant from time to time and was usually entertaining his employees and clients. The door of our home was never shut. I respected my father because he was strict but always fair and understanding. He was not an unreasonable person; he was a really good person, working hard, and he had a good relationship with the family.

My grandmother lived with us, and I think she almost 'kidnapped' me! I didn't see my family very much; I was always with my grandma. Whereas I have cherished memories of us walking in the hills, visiting her relatives on my father's side and friends on foot many miles away, I do not remember much about my mother or my siblings. When I was six or seven I had a devastating experience. My mother told me that my grandmother had died but I did not believe it, even though she was in her coffin. I thought she would wake up and was heartbroken when the coffin lid was closed. I thought that I was all alone in the entire universe, and even my early adulthood was tainted with grief. I couldn't overcome this grief for a very long time; we were close, very close.

I have never been a Buddhist – in fact I didn't believe in any religion. My father was an atheist, my mother was a Buddhist.

Obviously I was influenced by my mother, but because my grandma was more influential I was not so much in touch with my mother. My grandmother had a religion and believed in *Tenrikyo*, a Nara-based religious sect, and she used to take me to her local temple and occasionally to the one in a town. I didn't know about these things, about what she believed in, but in the room where we both slept she always had an altar and holy water. I saw her praying, and I sat next to her and, even though I didn't know anything, I bowed and things like that. But she left me the idea that there is God, so I knew there is God. I didn't know who is the God, but I knew I could talk to God. After my grandmother's death, I often spoke to "God" without knowing who He was.

Moving to Tokyo

I went to study in Tokyo because I wanted to speak English. Before I went to Junior High School I had a magazine my father used to buy each month, called *Shougakku Rokunen no Tomo*. It had included a free dictionary, an English-Japanese dictionary. Because I lived in the countryside I didn't know the outside world, but that simple dictionary opened a window so I was thrilled, so excited about it – I was about eleven or twelve years old. So I decided I will speak this language. This was to change my life!

I went to a prep school in Tokyo. Towards the end of the year, a lecturer came and he spoke beautiful English, and I thought, "This is the way I want to speak English!" After the lecture I waited and when he came out, I said, "I want to speak English like you do! But I'm bad at maths, so I can't go to this university". He said, "If you graduate from this university you still won't be able to speak English". I was so surprised! Then he said, "If you really want to be able to speak the language, go *to Nichi-Bei Kaiwa Gakuin* (American-Japanese Language Institute), and I know you will pass. If you graduate from this school you will be speaking English".

So that was in Tokyo, in Yotsuya. It was very, very hard. Lots of students go in, but you graduate in only two years and there are only two classes in the final year. Every Friday they have a test, changing the classes. Everybody went to the coffee shop afterwards and talked in Japanese, drinking coffee, eating cakes, and I thought, "I will never be able to learn English with this lifestyle!" So I found a babysitting job in Tokyo because I really wanted to speak English. I lived in with three small children, and looked after them after school and in this way I learnt English. They were a Dutch family, and they spoke beautiful English, so that way I could learn from them.

Converting to Christianity

It was while studying English in Tokyo I met my future husband Paul Holmes. He was working in a language school as well, making programmes, teaching, and he was also an English lecturer in a university. I met him through friends, I was in my late teens then, and after my graduation we were married and blessed with two sons. When I met Paul, he was a Christian, but he didn't say anything about that, and after we married, every Sunday morning, he asked me if he could go to Church - we did have a very simple wedding in a church. I wanted to sleep, so I said, "Yes, please go to Church". I had heavy anaemia then so it was hard to get up in the morning (I don't have it now). So he went and I stayed at home.

He was a very gentle man, and very humble, always appreciating things, being thankful for things, and very kind. And also he had joy, which I didn't have. I didn't have any of these things he had, the quality of his life, his character. I just admired him, and thought, "Why haven't I got this – this joy, this peace, this appreciation?" I envied his character and wanted to be like him but did not know how. And then one day it just dawned on me, "He goes to Church... I see!" So I thought it's something to do with that! Eventually I started going to Church. I became a Christian and I got baptised, but my life didn't change, you know. I was just the same – moody, critical and miserable. In the midst of my disappointment, Paul comforted and encouraged me. He said he loved me just as I was and did not need to change. One day as I was reading the Bible, I was transfixed by a verse from Isaiah 43:4 "You are precious in My sight, and I love you." I was to come across the verse many times – God's love is unconditional - I realised that God was speaking to me personally. I opened my heart to Him and He patiently started to change me.

I brought up my children in a Christian way, but it was very difficult, especially with Paul dying at such an early stage when we had been married nearly fifteen years. But they have a good memory of him. So that's how my Christian life came. Still I was not spiritually awakened, but after Paul died, I became stronger.

A new life in England

We moved to London from Japan in 1979. Life wasn't easy; Paul had to find a new job and our boys, eight and five, had to learn to speak English and settle down in their new schools. My mother-in-law, widowed young when Paul, an only child, was only thirteen, was living in London. While we were staying with her for three months, she dominated our household and I had to immediately set to work. The difficulties did not oppress me as I was determined to adjust to my new life whatever came up. Although our children soon picked up the language, they also experienced hardship at school and at Church because of their Japanese looks. In those years there was still blatant discrimination against foreigners in England. Dinner time used to be my mother-in-law's lecture time. She blamed Britain's decline on immigrants, especially from the Far East. My husband had not wanted me to work, he wanted me to support the house and so on, but his mother wouldn't have it; "If you don't work, you don't eat!" She was a very tough person, so even when we first came from Japan to live here, when we arrived in a taxi– we had to stay at her house – she said, "So you are going to work, what are you going to do?" I couldn't even count the money, and my English was terrible especially as I had studied American-English. So my husband and I decided that I should go and study at an English school for two years, to improve my English. Then my mother-in-law said, "But you have to learn English-English, so if you work, you'll learn!" I had to knock on all these shop doors, and she was always saying every day, "Haven't you got a job yet?" Eventually I worked in the Kanebo Cosmetics company, in the orders department. They were looking for people so I applied and got an interview. They said, "This is the last chance for Kanebo. If we get a good person we'll keep Kanebo; but we're losing money now, so we will finish". There were quite a lot of people who were doing interviews and wanted to get that job. And they said, "Can you sell?" I said, "I can sell anything!" So they gave me the job, and I really worked so very hard. I got lots and lots of customers and Kanebo shot up, I wore a Kimono from time to time. But once you start working, and you are earning money, and you are enjoying the job, you want to keep on working and getting better and better, so you see the family less. I think it was not a very good idea. The children were very small and I think they suffered quite a lot. You can't have both, you know. And then Kanebo sent me to Harrods, and I enjoyed being there very much. I was in Harrods when Paul died, in fact.

Paul was killed in a plane crash while on a business trip five years after we settled in London. In the darkest days of my life the Word of God sustained me. Even though I thought Jesus was speaking to me every day through the Bible, there were times when I could hardly face the day. One day Jesus spoke to me directly, saying, "My grace is sufficient for you, for My strength is made perfect in your weakness. I need you as much as you need Me. We will work together." I did not know what He meant then but I was somehow encouraged as I had thought I was nobody and had a huge void in my heart since Paul's death.

Teaching Japanese in England

This was in the 1980s and really I wanted to teach the Japanese language as I was trained to do that in Tokyo and had enjoyed helping people, even though I never had any paid employment in Japan. However, there was not much demand at that time. I put my name to the language schools, but no-one called.

Then, maybe two months after Paul died, a language school in London asked me to come two evenings a week to teach a businessman from an oil company, who would be seconded to their branch in Tokyo. Although I was still mourning and working during the day, I took the job praying that he wouldn't be a difficult person. In those days, tears used to gush out of the blue, and my heart would start beating violently and frighten me. I would have to run into the Ladies, wash my face and re-apply my makeup while I was working. Fortunately, the businessman was an English gentleman. Having noticed the fish pin on my collar, he told me that he too was a Christian. I was overwhelmed by God's kindness and cried. That was the first student; I left my daytime job, and the school gave me more and more students.

They were business people who had to go to Japan, the *crème de la crème* as it were. That was through the school, I did maybe two years with the language school, and then gradually I started my own school. I was teaching lots of different people for quite a long time, not only teaching the language but also interpreting and translating. Though the preparations took a longer time for each student, I thoroughly enjoyed the work and made text books for them. You learn a lot about your own language from both sides, learning English and teaching Japanese. I was successful too and thought that it was to be my lifetime's work.

First encounter with POW graves

Because I married an Englishman, my mother told me about a grave for British POWs. It was called "the Iruka Boys' Grave" in Japanese, and was about ten miles away near the copper mine. But between our home to Kiwa-cho - they called it Iruka then - there were lots of mountains, we had to walk a long way but my mother took us there. The grave was very simple, wood painted white, and they put the names in rows, with lots of stones to make it higher and they'd made a wooden cross. When I saw the grave for the first time I didn't feel anything very striking… I couldn't even imagine that British people were here, and I never could understand the War. I had two small children and a very busy time, so I didn't think very much about it.

Returning to Iruka

A few years after my husband's death, on a visit to my parents in Kiwa-Cho in about 1988, mother and I went to see the grave of sixteen British Prisoners of War. My mother had taken us to it when Paul and I were living in Tokyo with our two small boys. This time, the simple grave we had seen decades ago had been transformed into a beautiful marble memorial, with a Roll of Honour on the right hand side and the history of the war, especially of the Iruka POWs, explained on the left. There was a large wreath of orchids laid at the centre, and a large copper cross behind the memorial stone. I was touched by the local people who had built this Christian memorial site, even though they themselves were not Christians. After the mine had closed, people deserted the village for new employment and, decades on, mainly elderly people remained. I was amazed to see something so beautiful and so foreign in the midst of nowhere and wondered, "How had they built it?" I thought of the men who survived their ordeal, and of the mothers of the sixteen names on the roll of honour. Would they be comforted if I could find them and tell them about the grave? If my sons were taken away for the war and never came back, what would I have done? The beautiful wreath of orchids looked very expensive, and I wondered, "Who did this?" You know, they're still coming here and doing this. And then, just for a second in my mind I saw a vision of many people gathered there. I think God just gave me the vision because I was born there. So I thought if I told the people who were connected with this place, especially the mothers, that there's a beautiful memorial site, and people are looking after it, then they would be comforted.

So I took lots and lots of photos, and after I came to London I didn't know how to find these people connected with this, I just prayed for about a year, and suddenly something happened. My mother sent me a letter that Joe Cummings, who lived in Northumberland, had written to a Catholic priest who lived not too far, maybe ten miles or more in a different Wakayama city, in Shingu city. The Catholic priest had seen this memorial site, and he was so touched, he wrote about it in a Far Eastern Catholic magazine, and that Catholic magazine was given to Joe. The person who gave it to him asked him, "Is this about you? Is this about the place you were in?" He thought that because the name has been changed – *Iruka* into *Kiwa-cho* - he thought it was good to put them together.

Meeting Joe Cummings

Joe wrote to the Catholic priest thanking him for the article, and my mother sent it to me. From that letter I contacted Joe, and very fortunately Joe was an open-minded person. If he had been a different person this would never have happened. But he was so happy to know about the memorial site, and he told lots of people about it, but nobody believed him. Even when shown the photos they said, "No, the Japanese cannot do this kind of thing". So he asked me, "Can you send me more, photos, and more information?" After corresponding for about a year, Joe came to the Woodwork Exhibition in London and stayed at our house for a few days. He brought us some handmade gifts and taught Christopher, my younger son, about woodwork. Later, Danny, my older son, and I went to see Joe and Mona in Rothbury. Joe wanted to introduce us to the members of his local FEPOW (Far East Prisoners of War) club. But his idea was sharply refused. No FEPOWs wanted to meet any Japanese, nor believe that the memorial site in Kiwa-Cho existed.

Joe took us to meet Jimmy, his close friend who had shared his captivity in Thailand and Iruka, and his charming wife Edna. They lived in a settlement for those who had worked for Lord William Armstrong in Cragside. It was a beautiful place with a garden full of flowers in front of their terraced house. Jimmy and Edna welcomed us warmly and in a short while I felt a special bond towards them. I apologised to Jimmy for the atrocities he had suffered. Jimmy and Edna both said, "No, no, it was not your fault. You don't need to apologise." However, they seemed to be relieved to hear, "I am sorry." They did not tell us about their cruel treatment, but instead they spoke to us about the funny side of the war. Jimmy showed us a fan with both British and Japanese signatures. *Ishihara Sangyo*, the Iruka mine company, gave each prisoner of war a fan when they were freed. Some of the miners had been kind thus their names were recorded. Jimmy showed us some Japanese Thai money. Of the thousands of POWs captured in Singapore and sent to work on the notorious Thai-Burma railway, 300 were sent to Iruka after the completion of the railway.

"Actually, we volunteered to go as our doctor advised us to." Joe spoke. "Volunteered?"

"Yes, the doctor told us that Japan's weather would be more tolerable and that the chance of survival would be better there." Jimmy agreed.

Jimmy put a tiny stone in my palm. It was a copper ore which he had dug up in the mine and brought back to Britain just like Joe had done. Then he showed us the chopsticks he had used in Iruka. These items were their treasures. Joe had also kept similar memorabilia including a British flag, one of the many which local people had made from tissue paper to wave them goodbye as the POWs marched away from Iruka.

Cragside House

On a warm summer's day, Joe drove us to Cragside, now owned by the National Trust, where he was working as a volunteer guide. We went down a path shaded by flowering rhododendron bushes, to the entrance of the house. When we came to one particular room Joe got quite excited. Catching his breath, he explained that it was called the 'Japanese Room' because the Japanese Imperial family and dignitaries used to visit Cragside. In 1953, the then young Prince Akihito (the present Emperor of Japan) visited Cragside and stayed at the house for eight days, when he came for the Coronation of Queen Elizabeth II. Joe said, "You see, Keiko, Britain and Japan had been in a good relationship and even after the war our friendship carried on in Cragside."

Later in that afternoon, as we walked around Rothbury, we came across a POW who was on the Thai-Burma railway. After we were introduced to Jack, we chatted on the door step of the local newsagent for a while, and then, out of the blue, Jack invited us to his home. He told us that he had played tennis with Prince Akihito at Cragside. Later, Joe told us that Jack was one of the POWs who had vehemently refused to meet us at the FEPOW club.

Joe told me about the FEPOW Conference, to be held at the Barbican Centre in October.

"There will be more than a thousand people there from all over Britain, and beyond. I won't be going because it is rather far away for me and Jimmy." He said that it was an annual event which used to be held at the Royal Festival Hall but because of shrinking numbers had moved to the Barbican Centre. Joe also gave me the contact of Jane Flower, who lived in London and whose father was an officer in Thailand with Joe and Jimmy. According to Joe, Jane's father had died some years ago. "We called Jane's father 'two meter officer'. He was very tall." Joe and Jimmy told me many stories and spoke of Officer Flower with affection and respect. I was already excited when I thought of meeting many POWs and Jane at the conference.

FEPOW Annual Conference, 1991

October arrived. I was preparing to attend the FEPOW conference. But when I met Jane Flower prior to the conference, she said, "No, Keiko. You mustn't go!" I could not understand why she was so negative. "I am going," I said firmly. "Keiko, it's not the place for a Japanese to be. Joe is very different from most POWs. They are not like Joe at all." She looked worried, and it was becoming clear to me why she was against my attending the conference. She did not want me to get hurt but I was determined to attend. "If you go, they will eat you alive!" Jane added. She was a historian, writing an account of the Pacific War and interviewing thousands of POWs. She knew about POWs, I didn't.

A few days before the event, I rang the London FEPOW Club for a ticket. A lady answered the phone. As soon as I told her that I was Japanese her tone of voice changed and she started showering me with criticism against the Japanese. Then she passed the phone to a man, who was her husband and a POW. He repeated the things his wife had thrown at me. They did not really tell me where I could get a ticket for their event. I thought I would buy the ticket at the conference. (Some years later these people became good friends of mine, joined our pilgrimage, met several former Japanese soldiers and were reconciled in 1999). I prayed that God would open the door for me and that He would allow me to attend the conference. Jesus's answer was, "Let's go!"

By this time I had gathered some information about the Iruka memorial site and people who had known the prisoners. I flew to Japan several times visiting local government officials and the elderly people who looked after the site. My brother had taken over my father's business in 1979, and when my father retired he was eager to support me in my new mission. Fortunately, he knew some people who could talk about their experiences of the war and about the Iruka POWs.

One of my father's drivers got to know the POWs as a teenager working in the mine. He told me that there were some *hancho* (group leaders) who treated them kindly. Apparently, the mine owner who was an internationally minded person, because he had businesses overseas, told the miners to treat the POWs as human beings.

Talking to Mr Murakami, the elderly leader of the group looking after the grave, I was impressed by their compassion towards the Iruka POWs. As most Japanese people want their bodies/ashes to be buried in their homeland, they thought the POWs were the same. Therefore looking after their grave was the least they could do. When the previous simple grave was rebuilt in a better place, they 'collected the ashes of the POWs with tears'. He said, "They were the same ages as our sons. How much they'd wished to go home."

My brother allowed me to use his office to meet them. I had been compiling my interview pieces, and letters from Japan and Britain into a booklet, translating the English into Japanese and vice versa, and called it "Little Britain" after Rupert Brooke's poem. Though unfinished, I made ten copies and took them with me to the Barbican Centre, to the FEPOW conference.

I was the only Japanese there, the only one. I saw many elderly people gathered in the foyer of the concert hall, and was sure they were the POWs I had been longing to meet. I went up to a small group of people and introduced myself. But when I said I was Japanese, they became very indignant and shouted at me, saying, "Go away! We don't like Japanese!" "Get out!" "What are you doing here?" "What do you think we are?" and things like that.

I saw their angry eyes and then remembered the Word of God, "You are precious in My sight, and I love you." So I tried to show my little photo book called "Little Britain". I had the photos, and I showed them the memorial site, and a few people stopped, and some people went away. I had written in English and Japanese, essays of POWs. Some people thought, "Oh, Japanese can do this?" or, "All we hear about Japan are evil reports...". They were now seeing a different side of their enemies. I thought God wanted me to convey His love to people suffering from the scars of war, and I knew He wanted to heal them all.

Anyway, I still didn't have a ticket – but I was not going to leave without getting a ticket to go into the conference. This was all just in the foyer, but the people who had said "Go away" became friendlier, and invited me to sit with them while waiting for the door to open. I still hadn't bought a ticket, and when I explained my situation to them, they asked for a copy of my booklet each. I was delighted. As soon as I handed the booklets to them, they became enthusiastic, and one of them wrote a moving letter to me after the event.

Once I got it in, well, it was quite a heavy atmosphere; I felt their pain, and their anger. You know, their anger was pushed down, repressed, but there's anger, and their difficulties. I felt so much compassion, it just came. And I remembered the words, "We will work together", which God had said to me when my husband died. I knew then what He had meant. Somebody had to do something about the situation.

I began to think about how to get these people, the POWs, to go to Japan, but there were lots of difficulties. I thought, "Well, I have to do this, I *want* to do this", because I was born there. When I was growing up I didn't like the place, but there was a reason why I was born in that particular place; there was a reason why I married an Englishman, and why I am here in England. Looking back at the separation from my mother and the devastating death of my grandmother, I could see God's hand and he helped me to turn negative into positive. And I just prayed that God would use me for this purpose.

The Iruka Boys

I named the Iruka POWs 'Iruka Boys'. They liked it and started calling me 'Iruka girl'. By this time I was teaching Japanese at the Sumitomo Corporation. The company kindly allowed me to have access to photocopiers and other necessary facilities. I went to the office very early in the morning and copied and bound the booklets to send to POW clubs. My lawyer student, Richard, had 150 booklets made at his office and with the copies I was producing, could send it to more POWs. Their response was overwhelming. Some wrote to me that it was healing to read it.

I started fundraising for an Iruka Boys' pilgrimage to Japan. Even though they did not agree to visit Japan again I was certain that we could take at least five of them. I thought it was easy to raise funds for the cost of the pilgrimage, thinking that Japanese companies would heartily welcome this project. Although some companies were happy to help, many companies were not.

Some younger Japanese were not pleased and were saying, "What are you talking about? The War ended such a long time ago! What are you doing? Forget it!" They thought that I was anti-Japanese. How could such a simple thing have become so complicated?

In the meantime many Iruka Boys expressed an interest in joining the pilgrimage. Other POWs were indignant and told them that if they listened to Keiko Holmes and went to Japan for reconciliation, they would be ostracised. Many who said they would go to Japan the day before would say "No" the following day. This went on for a while. In the end about forty people decided to join. They thought that their war might end by visiting Japan and that they might be freed from nightmares. Jim from the Midlands wanted to thank the people who had erected and looked after the memorial site.

But there was still animosity against me amongst some POWs and a letter was circulating saying, "Keiko is not a Christian. She wants to throw us off our guard. She is a spy from the Japanese government." Stan, in a wheelchair, was one of those who believed the rumour and refused to talk to me. His friend finally persuaded him and Stan went to Japan, visiting a university, a school and other places including the Hiroshima Peace Park. Wherever he went they wanted to hear his story and apologise to him. He came back to England and stopped using his wheelchair.

One day, I came across the local newspaper cutting, which my brother had given me about a memorial service for the Iruka Boys in 1990. It had been attended by twenty-one men in their 60s who had been fifteen years old, when they, together with another seventy-nine, were sent to work in the mine by their school.

The paper reported that the men were missing the POWs. The memorial photo included the leader's name, Masao Okamuro, who was the director of the post office in Kumano City, about twenty-five kilometers from the shrine. I send him a letter with a copy of Little Britain and asked him to be involved in the project. He replied immediately and wrote, "Though I am not a Christian, I was touched by your faith, your care for the POWs and your affection for your homeland. We often talk about the 'Iruka Boys' and are missing them. I will have a meeting with my school friends to discuss your request and come back to you." A week later, another letter followed saying that his friends (15 of them) unanimously agreed to work with me.

Later, when I met Mr Okamuro and his school friends, they told me that they would watch with interest the Iruka Boys marching briskly to and from the mine. They looked gentlemanly and orderly. The young children had developed a love for them and wanted to exchange language lessons, even though the military personnel ordered them strictly not to go near the POWs. When the guards were not around, the children and the POWs exchanged language lessons.

Iruka Boys' Pilgrimage of Reconciliation

In 1992 I took the first pilgrimage of the 'Iruka Boys', as they were to be known, to Japan. There were about 26 of them, plus myself and somebody else to be with them. It had been such a difficult time to get money together, and then get people to agree to go, but we made it happen.

When we stepped from the train on to the platform of Kumano City station, anxious Mr Okamuro rushed towards us with a Union Jack in his hand. The entrance and front of the station were packed with welcoming people waving Union Jacks and Japanese flags. Some girls had bouquets in their arms and a little girl was in a beautiful kimono holding an elderly man's hand. She was a former school child's granddaughter. There was a sea of flashing lights with films and photos being taken of the Iruka Boys' arrival. Some people had pens and papers, some tape recorders. Everybody was excited. The Iruka Boys were overwhelmed by the Japanese people's enthusiastic welcome. Eventually we settled in the Japanese inn by the lush green Toro gorge in Kiwa-Cho.

Welcome receptions were held almost every day. These were organised by local government officials, the press group, the elderly people's group who had been looking after the memorial site, the Lions Club and the town committee. The Iruka Boys were asked to give speeches which were interpreted by some volunteers from Tokyo and Osaka. Many Iruka Boys were from the

Northumberland and Newcastle area and people could not understand their accent, but they thought that I could! I had been so occupied in raising funds, communicating with the Iruka Boys, being interviewed and organising the event with Mr Okamuro while teaching Japanese. Giving speeches and translating speeches of both sides had not occurred to me!

The sixteen Iruka Boys' Memorial Service was attended by many local people and dignitaries of Mie Prefecture and Kumano City, Kyoto, Osaka, Nagoya and Tokyo – the place was packed. The attendance of Fred, the former interpreter, of the POWs from Kyoto delighted the Iruka Boys, especially the vicar Richard White who was given a Bible by him in those difficult times. The pocket Bible from Fred was Richard's treasure. People started to call the Iruka memorial site "Little Britain". Throughout our visit to Japan, because of the media coverage, many people recognised us, and often rushed towards us and apologised saying, *'Gomen nasai, gomen nasai'* (I am sorry) holding the Iruka Boys' hands tight with affection.

What an amazing, eye-opening and life-changing ten days in Japan! The friendship and care they received was overwhelming, and the Iruka Boys would say, "No more nightmares!" "I've laid the ghost and I am free!" "Friendship is better than gold." Their wives told me that their husbands had been changed and that it had become easier to live with them. They also asked me to continue the reconciliation work not only taking Iruka POWs but also other POWs to Japan.

After the first expedition, which was extraordinary for those people, we did another one the following year, but only one person went – I couldn't make it, but I sent one person, the son of an Iruka Boy. In Japan they looked after him, and he walked miles and miles to the copper mine, from the train station, because he wanted to experience what the father had to do. So he walked miles. He was really happy, and lots of local people gathered, and people looked after him very well. Then the following year fourteen of us went, with different people.

Reconciliation and overcoming taboos

Back in the 1990s it was almost taboo to speak about the war. But now when we visit, the POWs go to schools, visit universities, churches, and many different organisations. So we mix with lots of people, even Buddhist people invite us, and some Buddhist temples give us accommodation. The first group called themselves "The Pioneers", they met some of their Japanese counterparts as well, and some people apologised. The Burma Campaign Japanese people, they didn't know anything about this, they apologised in Kyoto. Many people came, and they apologised. Wherever we go, people say, "Oh, the Iruka Boys!" and they come and say, "Sorry, *Gomen nasai, gomen nasai!*". It's interesting that the people themselves come and apologise, but the government does not. The government and politicians are living in a different world.

When the Iruka Boys go to Japan even Japanese ex-soldiers come and apologise; they are not prompted, they do that themselves. Even in England one former Japanese ex-soldier came, and to my surprise, was on the floor in apology. Everyone was saying, "Please, get up," and hugging him, and so on. It's different every time for the POWs and on the Japanese side, some people are frightened because they thought it would be a kind of revenge. But lots of local people are so happy to see these POWs. I think it was healing for them, for the Japanese as much as for the British POWs. Now I think it's getting easier because the people want to know what happened, they want to know what went on. Many people are helping us now, and without their help we couldn't do it. There are a lot of people in Tokyo, Kumano, Kyoto, Hiroshima, we used to have Nagasaki as well, and Hirado, - in many places people host the Iruka Boys in their homes, push their wheelchairs, and help them get around.

Agape World

Our charity's name 'Agape' was chosen in 1996. It is a Greek word meaning unconditional love. However, because many organisations use 'Agape', we eventually changed it to 'Agape World'. I am only the representative of this, and many other people are working with this charity. The Bible tells us that, 'There is no fear in Love'. If I have this love for others, I thought, I could go anywhere and meet anyone. Whatever situation I might face, I would not be hurt.

More and more POWs became interested in visiting Japan as they heard about our work from theIruka Boys. They also joined our fundraising events, some coming down to London and staying at my house. More Japanese companies started to help through the positive media reports. After our third successful pilgrimage, I met Mr Hiroaki Fujii, the then-Ambassador to the UK. Having compassion towards the POWs, he arranged for the Japanese government to support us. Gradually numerous Japanese companies joined. This continued for eleven years, and Sumitomo Europe, who let us use one of their beautiful office rooms, sustained us until March 2010. In 1993, when I was organising the third pilgrimage, Mr Nishikawa, then the director of Sumitomo Europe, knocked on my office door and asked if we could make it to Japan. He introduced the person in charge of All Nippon Airways (ANA) who gladly supported us for many years. Now Japan Air Lines are helping us. The Japanese Embassy continues to host much-appreciated Reconciliation Receptions which all enjoy and look forward to each year.

When we received charity status the late Sir Peter Parker kindly took up the post of patron, as promised. Understanding our need, he encouraged his associated companies to support us. After pilgrimages, the POWs wrote their thank you letters to Sir Peter and always received a personal reply from him.

Responses to Reconciliation visits

Since 1992 about 500 POWs from Britain and other nations have participated in our pilgrimages and met their former perpetrators, who came to our events and apologised. The POWs would forgive them and they were reconciled. By asking for forgiveness, the former Japanese soldiers were released from their conscience, guilt and sorrow, and POWs, by forgiving, were freed from anger, grudge, and suffering. Many volunteers joined us from different parts of Japan and by pouring out their love for the POWs were blessed by seeing that. They have been arranging visits to kindergartens, schools, universities and different organisations. Children welcome the POWs with Union Jacks and ask innocent questions, and promise them that they would eat what their mothers gave them at meal times. They are always sincerely listened to by university students, and actively participate in the discussions. POWs would ask them to go into politics and make a peaceful world. Numerous church ministers have been organising special reconciliation services and apologised on their knees with their congregations. Touched by their affection and sincerity, POWs hug and kiss them, forgiving all. Whenever we travel to the Hiroshima or Nagasaki Peace Parks and learn about the catastrophic disasters, some of the POWs and their families ask for forgiveness for the West. Hiroshima volunteers also learn about Japan's atrocities and realise they are not the only victims of the war, and because both sides went through the dire experiences, they become bonded together.

Many people worked with us for a period of time in London and in Japan. Vicar David Busk was responsible for the Nagasaki area until recalled to England. Keiko in the Kanto area, Tokio in Kumano, Mariko in Kyoto, and Naoko and Koshi in the Hiroshima area have been our main leaders. As well as Christians there are Buddhists, Shinto believers, atheists, and people of other faith all knitted together by a special thread. In the course of time, many POWs who had believed the rumour that I was a spy from the Japanese government and tried hard to stop others joining us, eventually came to Japan and forgave the Japanese. In London, apart from our trustees we have Harue, who joined three years ago and is very popular with POWs and their families. They all work with me with passion. Quite recently Kaz, whose wife is English, started helping us with translation work. Many people continue to pray for us, too. Although POWs are passing away, their families are encouraging us to keep going. POWs, civilian internees and their families, as well as 'Comfort women' have visited Japan with us. Agape World also visits other Far Eastern countries deeply affected by the war.

Royal Encounters and Honours

Having been awarded the OBE in Windsor Castle by H.M. the Queen in 1998, I was invited to a state banquet at Buckingham Palace with my son Chris, in the same year. The Queen, the Japanese Emperor and Empress, and the Queen Mother were welcoming over 100 guests. The Queen greeted me in a friendly manner saying, "Oh, we meet again!" The Emperor and the Empress were very pleased with the work that Agape World had been doing, and thanked me sincerely. I met them several times during their state visits in 1998 and in 2012, and was impressed by their humility. During our pilgrimage in 2000, I was invited with my other son Daniel to the Imperial Palace by the Empress. The Empress Michiko spent one whole hour with us, much more than was usual. My son and I we were deeply moved by how much she cared for the POWs.

Reflections

I know I have been a very determined person in life, one way or another; if I decide I want to do something, I will do it. Even if everybody's gone from that era of the War, there are sons and daughters and grandchildren, so it's better to do something to help them than nothing.

Sometimes when people ask me, "Which country would you prefer to live in?" I reply that I love both England and Japan. When I travel to Japan it appeals to me, at the same time when I come back to England, I say to myself, "This is my home". I hope that I can continue to live here, I love to live in England, but if God tells me to live in Japan, I'll obey Him. Without faith in Christ, I would not have done anything.

Agape World is eternally grateful to all those who, in Japan and England, have worked with us. We needed, and received, support from some extraordinary people, just in time. Many are still with us, endeavouring as a team, focused on our vision, our special assignment. I am especially grateful to the Okamuro group who took up the daunting but exciting challenge of this adventure at the very beginning of our pilgrimages, and shared the great joy and gratitude, saying, "Keiko's God did it!"

KEIKO HOLMES OBE

Founder of Agape World for P.O.W. Reconciliation and Humanitarian Work

	Born in Kiwa-Cho, Kumano City, Mie Prefecture, Japan
1960s	Studied English at the American Japanese Language Institute in Tokyo; met and married Paul Holmes while studying in Tokyo
1970s	First saw Kiwa-Cho memorial site to the Iruka POWs
1979	Moved to London with her family; worked in several places
1984	Death of husband Paul in an air accident; started teaching Japanese language to business people
1986	Started own Japanese language business in London
1988	Revisited Iruka memorial site and contacted a Far East Prisoner of War in Northumberland
1991	Attended Far Eastern Prisoners of War (FEPOW) conference in London
1992	Lead the first Pilgrimage of Reconciliation – the 'Iruka Boys' – to the memorial site at Kiwa-Cho; subsequent tours of FEPOWs to Japan gain momentum and support
1994	Summer Celebration: started bringing Japanese supporters and POWs to London for friendship events
1996	Reconciliation programme named 'Agape', later renamed 'Agape World'
1998	Keiko was acknowledged by the Japanese Emperor and Empress during their state visit to London when they met at the State Banquet at Buckingham Palace with HM the Queen
2000s	Approximately two trips a year to Japan were organised by Agape World, with nearly 500 ex-POWs,

internees and their families coming from the UK, the Netherlands, Australia, and Canada

Reconciliation work with other Far Eastern countries affected by the War started by visiting their countries; an Annual Service of Reconciliation held at Kensington Temple Church in London

2015   Agape World's work continues to expand into other Far Eastern countries in order to promote friendship and understanding between former FEPOWs and their families and the Japanese people, including other POWs, 'Comfort women', and civilian internees affected by the War.

HONOURS

1996   Given The Japan Society Award for her work in Anglo-Japanese Reconciliation

1998   Conferred OBE by HM Queen Elizabeth II in recognition of her work in fostering Anglo-Japanese Reconciliation

1999   Given Foreign Ministry Award by the Japanese Government

2000   Given title of Companion of the Cross of Nails by Coventry Cathedral on 18th August

POW Stanley (in wheelchair) at the Peace Park, Hiroshima c.1998

PHOTOGRAPHIC CAPTIONS & CREDITS

All portraits and cover design by Jeremy Hoare

Page 21   Sir Hugh Cortazzi at the Oriental Club, London May
           1991
           Jeremy Hoare

Page 41   Phillida Purvis with Solar Lighting project in Uganda
           2015
           courtesy of P Purvis

Page 57   London School of Economics, Houghton Street, London
           Jeremy Hoare

Page 76   Professor Bownas's publications on Japanese Verse
           courtesy of W Cook Bownas

Page 89   Joji Hirota performing with his female Taiko Group,
           2013
           Suzanne Perrin

Page 110   Hatch Mill Hospice Japanese garden, Farnham 2013
           Jeremy Hoare

Page 123   Junko Kobayashi practising at home, 2011
           Jeremy Hoare

Page 144   The Nichi-Ei Times 1991-2002, and other books by
           Setsuo Kato
           courtesy of S Kato

Page 167   Ondorisha knitwear catalogue c.1948
           courtesy of T Watanabe

Page 191   POW Stanley (in wheelchair) at the Peace Park,
           Hiroshima c.1998
           courtesy of K Holmes

SUZANNE PERRIN B.A. (Hons), M.A.

is an independent researcher and historian specialising in Japanese History, Art & Culture, and founded **Japan Interlink** in 1995 to promote the understanding of Japan in the UK through educational and cultural events.

Suzanne studied *Nihonga* traditional Japanese painting at Nagoya University of Arts and gives lectures and courses on a wide range of Japanese subjects to universities including the University of London Institutes, museums including the British Museum and the V&A Museum, and to NADFAS in the UK, AADFAS in Australia, DARTS in South Africa, and the University of Cape Town.

Suzanne has published many articles on traditional and contemporary aspects of Japan, including Japanese architecture, gardens and lifestyle, and 'greening' the environment. She visits Japan on a regular basis to continue her research.

Cultural Director
Japan Interlink London

www.japaninterlink.com

info@japaninterlink.com

JEREMY HOARE

After a career in UK network television as a cameraman and lighting director, Jeremy became a travel photographer and has visited over sixty countries. His photographs are published worldwide from thousands of images selling through photo libraries.

Jeremy founded the online **Kyoto Photo Gallery** in 2014 and has had several photo exhibitions connected with Japan in London, Kyoto and Tokyo.

He has authored one book, *Through the Viewfinder* published by Entertainment Technology Press in 2008 for people aiming to be professional TV cameramen.

Jeremy is a member of the British Guild of Travel Writers and is on the judging panel of the prestigious international Travel Photographer of the Year competition.

His partner, Chizuko Kimura, is a kimono maker and Urasenke tea master.

www.kyotophotogallery.com

www.jeremyhoare.com